Lady Glenconner

Manners & Mischief

An A-Z of a Life Lived Well

First published in the UK in 2025 by Bedford Square Publishers Ltd,
London, UK
This paperback edition published in the UK in 2026

bedfordsquarepublishers.co.uk

A CIP catalogue record for this book is available
from the British Library.

Internal illustrations by Philippa Gist ©

ISBN
978-1-83501-578-0 (Paperback)
978-1-83501-467-7 (Hardback)
978-1-83501-468-4 (eBook)

2 4 6 8 10 9 7 5 3 1

Typeset by Palimpsest Book Production Ltd, Falkirk, Stirlingshire

Printed in Great Britain by CPI Group (UK) Ltd, Croydon CR0 4YY

The manufacturer's authorised representative in the EU for
product safety is Easy Access System Europe, Mustamäe tee 50,
10621 Tallinn, Estonia
gpsr.requests@easproject.com

Manners & Mischief

To my beloved sisters Carey and Sarah

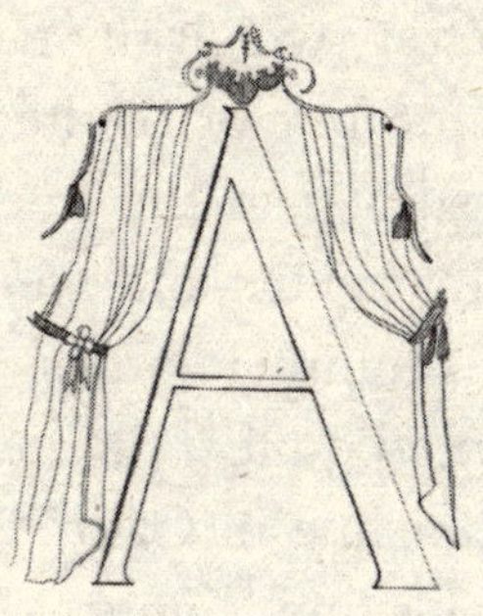

Affair

The other day I made the most extraordinary discovery. My mother had a tiny little writing case, which had a very stiff lock that I had never been able to open. My daughter, Amy, was staying with me and managed to prise open the lock, and inside found letters written by Queen Elizabeth to my mother as well as rather heartbreaking letters which Charles had written to her from school. It was fascinating reading through these, but then underneath them all, wrapped in brown paper, was a little book that turned out to be a diary my father had kept whilst he was in Cairo where he was stationed with the Scots Guards during the war. My mother went with him and worked with the Red Cross there. I had seen earlier letters which my father had written home describing the horror of the war, standing in newly dug out foxholes in the freezing cold desert every night, only his helmet and eyes visible, scouring the landscape for Rommel and his advancing army. But the diary painted quite a different picture of life away from the front line in Cairo. It was a world of champagne cocktails and dinner at the Continental or Shepheard's Hotel, perhaps going on to the Dugout cabaret, or to Jules' nightclub. There were polo and golf matches, picnics at the pyramids, dinner parties, even shooting parties. But the real surprise was the revelation that my father was having a cracking affair with a woman he refers to as 'M' and whom he writes passionately about. She was a secretary working for one of the generals and clearly because of their affair was always late to work. My father seemed frightfully worried about her and writes about going into the office to plead her case to ensure she didn't get into trouble. What is so extraordinary is that it all seems to have gone on in full view of everyone. He writes about one evening's dinner party at Shepheard's Hotel with a group of people including my mother and 'M', going on to Jules' nightclub: 'danced, sipped brandy and ginger ales. Gerald Grosvenor took Eliz home! Took M home. Flat. Bed by 5am'. I have no idea whether my mother (Eliz) had an affair with Gerald Grosvenor, but it's clear she must have known all about what was going on between my father and 'M'. And it paints a picture which is a world apart from the rather formal life they were leading in England.

I think this is what war does to people, the effect of being at the front and dealing with the potential imminence of death, makes life suddenly seem worth grabbing with both hands. I also think there is something that happens in the heat, particularly to those people who have been previously trussed up in boned and cumbersome underwear and who are suddenly free to wear lacy knickers and cotton dresses. It must have produced a sense of freedom and living from day to day, I think it got the blood pumping. I had never seen this passionate side of my father before. He buys 'M' jewellery before he leaves and writes of feeling desperate and depressed when he had to say goodbye to her before embarking on the long sea journey home. His diary of the voyage is peppered with notes of the times he sent her letters and telegrams.

My parents' marriage survived, I suspect, largely due to the intervention of my Great Aunt Bridget, a Christian Scientist, who clearly told my mother to put the events of the war behind her, patch things up and get on with trying to produce a son and heir for Holkham. My mother's diaries record that trying to get pregnant was not a joyful experience, but they managed it and of course went on to have my sister Sarah, so sadly the issue of an heir was unresolved.

They seem to work out how to carry on afterwards, and I think were reasonably happy; my father adored Holkham and my mother started Holkham pottery and threw herself into that. They were so young when they met, my mother was just fifteen and father was seventeen, so they were childhood sweethearts and just nineteen and twenty-one when they married. In those days they would certainly not have slept together before marriage and had no other experience of love or relationships. I suppose the same was true of my generation. I do think it's probably a mistake to marry so young and to the first person you fall in love with. Ideally, I believe you should have the opportunity to meet lots of people and have plenty of relationship experience before deciding who to spend your life with.

Amateur Dramatics

In amateur dramatics, as in most areas of my life up until the last few years, my role was strictly a supporting one to my husband Colin and Princess Margaret. The impetus and inspiration for the various plays we all put on, particularly at Glen in the Scottish Borders, came from Colin, and from Princess Margaret when she was staying. She and Colin used to love plotting sketches and songs to be performed, usually in front of a captive audience of people from the village who Colin had instructed to attend. We had an eclectic store of costumes which Colin had bought when we were in Hollywood, including some large plastic bottoms, which he had shipped back to England. I have a photograph of Princess Margaret dolled up in a fantastic dress as Mae West. Luckily, when the Queen first saw it in the *Daily Mail* she loved it and was very amused. And I also remember Princess Margaret singing the 'Chattanooga Choo Choo' wearing a Victorian dress and bonnet with Roddy Llewellyn following on behind. A lot of these things she enjoyed even more because Roddy, who was also very enthusiastic, was there.

I was never allowed to take part in the drama, my role was strictly behind the scenes, sewing on buttons and helping people into their costumes. It was very much Colin and Princess Margaret driving these events. I did sometimes hope they might say, 'Oh, Anne, why don't you be so and so in this play?' and give me a role, but they never did. I think it's one reason why I am rather enjoying my time in the limelight now, not as an actor but invited to give talks and be interviewed, finally I'm allowed to take centre stage.

My love of 'Am Dram' started during the war when my sister Carey I were sent up to Scotland to stay with Great Aunt Bridget. Her home, Cortachy Castle had been requisitioned and was being used as a hospital for Polish officers. We believed it was a very important part of our war work to keep the Polish officers entertained and so would put on little shows for them. Given that we were aged five and seven, and their English was not fantastic, I'm not at all sure quite how entertaining they found the perform-ances they were made to sit through!

Art

My father was rather surprised and horrified by the fact that my mother was a fan of the artist Beryl Cook. Her work was considered rather vulgar, and quite the opposite of some of the wonderful pictures on the walls at Holkham. But my mother bought several of her paintings and got to know the artist personally. The Queen Mother also seemed to enjoy Beryl Cook as I have a letter she wrote to my mother thanking her for the 'kitchen lunch' she had enjoyed with my mother at Holkham, 'eating delicious food, gossiping and laughing' and 'surrounded by those splendid ladies with their enormous arms and legs'. They were very good friends and from her letters I can see that the Queen Mother really valued the closeness of her friendship to my mother. I still have a couple of her Beryl Cook pictures, although my real love was for Victorian paintings, particularly the Pre-Raphaelites. I was never artistic unlike my mother and sister, but I enjoyed going to exhibitions. When I was married, even in London we had a staff of five or six, so we had a lot of spare time. We all took up working for various charities but had plenty of time to meet friends for lunch every day. Quite often someone would suggest going to see an exhibition in the afternoon, for example if something nice was on at the V&A we'd pop off and spend a happy afternoon wandering round the galleries.

When I was in New York, being interviewed by Tina Brown for *Lady in Waiting*, I received an invitation from a curator at the Metropolitan Museum of Art inviting me to go and see the painting 'The Wyndham Sisters' by John Singer Sargent which they had recently rehung. *The Times* had labelled the painting 'The greatest picture of modern times' and the Met rehang had placed it in a smallish room where it was very much the main event. It's a very large work in which Pamela Wyndham who was by then Pamela Tennant, Colin's grandmother, takes centre stage, reclining on a chaise-longue with one sister at her head and another at her feet. She was very beautiful and rather glamorous and was at the heart of the political and cultural establishment at the time. She went on to have five children with Colin's grandfather Edward Tennant, who became Lord Glenconner. She wasn't an easy person, famously needing to be the centre of attention, which, as I stood to have my photograph taken in front of the painting, I hoped was not a character trait common to all Lady Glenconners!

Basil's Bar

When Colin met Basil Charles on St Vincent and asked him to come to Mustique to run a bar, it was one of the most successful appointments he made. Basil has great charm and was brilliant with people. He made the bar the party hub of the island and it was, and is, a great success. He also cut a glamorous figure and attracted all the single ladies Colin invited to come to the island in the early days. He ended up falling in love with Lady Royston when she visited following the death of her husband and they lived together on the island for over ten years with her two children. He was also really kind to Colin, and when he left Mustique for St Lucia, took him on holiday once to Bali. Whilst Colin ended up burning through his inheritance, Basil ended up making a very good living from the bar, becoming rich and a celebrity in his own right. I saw him the last time I went to Mustique with another lovely lady in tow, and he cooked us the most delicious lobster and made his signature Mustique Mule. Basil was even asked to recreate his bar at The Goring Hotel near Buckingham Palace. They commissioned a bespoke driftwood bar and shipped in tons of sand and two coconut trees and had a steel band on hand – a little slice of Mustique in Belgravia. Pippa Middleton held a birthday party there as Basil had become great friends with the Middletons in Mustique and was invited to Prince William and Kate's wedding. He was also given an OBE for his services to underprivileged children's education as he had set up a wonderful education foundation, which awards scholarships to fund secondary education for deserving children on St Vincent and the Grenadines.

Baths

I know lots of people prefer showers but for me there's always the worry about one's hair and I love nothing more than a luxurious bath, especially if you're feeling a bit chilly. However, I've recently fractured my back, and the trouble is the older you get the more difficult it is to get out of a bath. My best friend Margaret Vyner unfortunately got stuck in her bath and thought she was going to die in it. She knew her cleaner wasn't coming for another two days and although she could hear her telephone ringing in her bedroom she couldn't get to it. Luckily her half-sister wondered why she wasn't picking up the telephone and asked Margaret's grandson to pop over and check on her. She was found just in time, the doctor said if she had been left another two hours she would have died. We were all appalled and terrified by this and for a time I would always take my telephone with me to the bath so I could call for help if I did get stuck. It's not something you think about when you are younger, but I had been heaving myself out of the bath using an elbow and one hand and I wonder whether that weakened my back and has led to my fracture. My daughters and daughter-in-law quite rightly said, 'That's the last time you are heaving yourself out of the bath,' and now we've installed this lovely electric chair which goes in and out of the bath. It makes the whole thing much easier and I feel more confident about being able to enjoy my bath again.

I think the Queen enjoyed her baths too. I remember once when Princess Margaret and I had been swimming in the pool at Buckingham Palace, which we did most mornings, she asked me if I'd like to go and have a look at the rooms where the Queen lived. Of course I jumped at the chance, and was shown a very charming bedroom, but what really struck me was the line of celluloid ducks wearing crowns lined up in order of size on the side of the bath.

Beauty

I don't spend a great deal on beauty products, I pretty much depend on the Boots No.7 range of skincare, and I'm amazed by the money that is spent on products these days. When I was younger I had acne, and I remember my mother taking me to 'a wonderful lady in London' to try and sort out the problem. The firm was run by two women who had been to Paris, which was seen as the centre of the beauty industry, to learn about creams and skincare. They gave me a cream which I still have the remnants of today and it's absolutely wonderful. It contains whale oil so you couldn't buy it now but I still use it, and people do comment that I have a very good complexion so I think it works. When I was young, we were never taught how to apply make-up, any emphasis on your personal appearance was thought to be the height of vanity and not acceptable, despite the need to always look presentable and tidy. I do remember the joy, however, of escaping to the cloakroom during dances where the cloakroom ladies were on hand to provide a safety pin or hairspray, and you could apply your lipstick and spend a few moments brushing your hair and relaxing with the other girls before returning to the agony of the ballroom and the anxious wait to be asked to dance.

In later life however, I've been asked to appear on various television shows and I adore the hair and make-up before going on. I've become extremely partial to false eyelashes – always single, never strips. I appeared on *Loose Women* the day before the launch party for my book *Picnic Papers* and was desperate my wonderful false lashes would still be in place for the party. I think I hardly slept that night with trying not to dislodge them.

I've also only ever worn Chanel Number 5 scent. I don't use it every day, only when I'm going out, but I always think I have a better time when I'm wearing it. Marilyn Monroe famously said when asked in an interview for *Life* magazine what she wore at night: 'I just wear Chanel Number 5.' I'd love to be that glamorous but I'm very fond of my cosy nightie in bed.

Boarding School

I was sent to Downham School in Essex to board aged eleven. I was incredibly homesick and rather resentful as my parents had only returned from Egypt the year before, so I didn't want to have to leave them again, but off I was sent with my leather trunk. The school was run by Mrs Crawford who lived with the under-mistress Miss Graham; it seems obvious to me now that they were partners, but I think at the time no one realised it. There were dreadful double standards then. I remember when Radclyffe Hall's book *The Well of Loneliness* was found in the library there was a terrific row, lesbianism was simply not allowed or acknowledged. If a girl was caught under the covers with another girl she was given a warning and if caught twice she would be expelled. So if you went to comfort someone who was homesick and crying in the dorm you had to make sure you stayed on top of the covers if you gave her a hug.

People often ask how you survive boarding school, and I think it's all about the friends you make there.

Somehow being thrown together with all these other girls, who are also homesick, created a real bond and many of the friends I made at school were friends for life. But I think to send off small children, aged seven or eight, really isn't on and I was very pleased when the Princess of Wales decided to send George to a day school. It's too young to be torn away from your parents. I think I was forced to grow up too early when my parents left me aged seven to go to Cairo, and the same thing applies to boarding school at that age. My daughter sent her children to a day school, and it was only when they asked to board aged thirteen that they went away, at that point they loved it. However, boarding school is now so incredibly expensive, I think it's only an option available to the very few.

Careers

I do worry sometimes that everybody these days thinks that they need to go to university. Of course, it's brilliant for some people but even if you have been to university there aren't always jobs afterwards and some people aren't suited to it. My grandson Euan was very clever and went to university, but he really did not enjoy it and his mother very sensibly said, 'You're very good with numbers and physics why don't you train as an electrician?' So he did and it's been a huge success, he's a first-rate electrician and very well paid. We need skilled plumbers, carpenters and electricians and I really do think more young people, girls and boys, might find that sort of work suits them better rather than pushing themselves through a degree which might not even lead to a job at the end of it all.

Charity

When I married Colin we lived in a very smart house in London and had a butler, cook, nanny and nursery maid and yet I thought I was terribly busy. It was expected of people like me to take one or two charities under one's belt to support and give our time to. I worked with a number of charities, including one that became Refuge, which provides safe houses for victims of domestic violence. If a woman could get away to a phone box there was a number she could call and if I was on duty I would go to the phone box, pick her up with her children and take them to a safe address. Heartbreakingly, they would often call at night and just be in their night-clothes. At the time I found it hard to understand why some of the women we had helped to escape quite often returned to their abuser, but subsequently of course I have a much greater empathy towards the complexity of these relationships.

There was also an obligation to look after the people who lived on your estate and worked for you, and at one time there were around six hundred cottages on the Holkham Estate. We partly funded the cottage hospital at Wells before the creation of the NHS, a practice that extended to other stately homes around the country, and would pay for the treatment of any workers who fell ill. We'd visit their cottages on the estate, taking baskets of food and stopping to have a cup of tea. Looking after the workers was something which Colin continued when we were in Mustique, where we built a new village and a church for the people who were living there. I used to teach in the school we built on the island, and if there were bright children we would pay for them to go to school on St Vincent. Colin also used to pay for some of the young men to go to England if they wanted to enrol in the army or the police. Before we arrived, it wasn't possible to be buried on the island but when we built the church the land there was consecrated and could then be used as a graveyard.

I can't do as much now but I'm very involved with fundraising for the church in my village and in helping to get it ready for events like weddings and funerals. I think wherever you are it's important to be aware of the world around you and do what you can to help in some way, in addition to being useful it's also personally really enjoyable and fulfilling.

Children

After the war my friends and I all longed to have large families and had a passion for having babies. What we really wanted was to try to give our children the childhood that the war and its aftermath had prevented us from enjoying. I think my mother thought we spoilt our five children, but I was so desperate that they would have experiences I hadn't been able to enjoy, like travelling and eating nice food. When the children were growing up we used to take them to a different capital city each holiday; we were lucky that we were able to afford to show them Paris, Berlin, Rome and other exciting cities. They tell me now that in the main, they had a happy childhood, which is what you hope to give your children.

I really loved my three sons, but I did always long for a daughter so going on to have twin girls was a real thrill. Now I'm older, my daughters and my daughter-in-law have all been amazing looking after me. I think the thing is that, after boys are married you don't see them so much, but girls seem to stay closer to their mother. Also having no brother, I was more used to girls, I loved my father, but he was rather distant and difficult, whereas my mother was fun and we adored her.

It was such a different time when I had children, I really only saw them in the morning when they came into my bedroom as I was having breakfast before Nanny whisked them away, and then again in the evening when they were brought in to see us before they were taken away to be bathed. And I have huge regrets about a very unkind nanny I had in the early days for the boys. I had no idea she was so awful until I was told by a lovely Spanish lady who was also working for us and could see what was going on. I sacked her immediately but still feel terrible about the impact she may have had, especially as I too had suffered at the hands of a cruel nanny. In the end we had our lovely nanny Barbara Barnes who had been brought up at Holkham and was absolutely wonderful for the youngest children. She went on to look after William and Harry until Diana became jealous of how fond they were of her and got rid of her. Barbara is still one of my closest friends and I'm forever grateful to her. I never thought of trying to raise my children differently to the way I was brought up. Today men play a much bigger part in children's lives, changing nappies and giving real practical help. Back then, Colin would play with the children but that was it and I didn't expect anything more than that as my father had never been very involved in our lives. In a way I had to focus all my energies on Colin who was prone to the same terrible tantrums as a toddler, he was like my grown-up child and required constant attention.

I do worry that children have a lack of boundaries these days, it sometimes feels as though adults have lost control of their children, not knowing where they are, letting them sit on their phones and not talk to people. I don't know whether it's because when we were young we were dealing with the war and really serious issues of life and death that made us perhaps grow up more quickly and be prepared to listen to figures of authority. I think it certainly made us more resilient. All children need love and encouragement, but I think they need boundaries too.

Cinema

Going to the cinema used to be a huge treat. When I was a child living at Holkham in Norfolk, we were very near a town called Wells-next-the-Sea which had a cinema where the programme changed twice a week. We used to cycle in with my mother from Holkham to see whatever was on. The cinema had a wonderful hidden organ which used to rise up slowly as the curtains went back and the screen was revealed, with the organist sitting there playing whatever tune accompanied the film. I loved the whole occasion of it and have continued to adore going to the cinema.

Princess Margaret also loved the escape which cinema provided. We sometimes used to make rather covert trips to the smokers' balcony at the Coronet cinema in Notting Hill to watch a matinee. Two of her favourite films were *Bonnie and Clyde* with Faye Dunaway and Warren Beatty, and later on *Thelma and Louise*. It's interesting that they were both films about escaping from or upending societal expectations.

Clothes

I've always loved clothes, partly I think because being brought up in the war and relying on coupons, the most we could expect was perhaps a pair of shoes when the existing pair were much too small, or the occasional new jumper. I grew rather fast and felt that was a real black mark against me as I needed new clothes and shoes at a time when they were hard to come by. We never had any nice clothes during the war and even afterwards it wasn't easy to find and afford anything new. When I 'came out' into society, there was a worry about what I would wear to my own coming out dance and I ended up wearing a dress made from a silk parachute given by an American officer which had been dyed green.

I've recently come across some of the letters my mother was sent by the Queen when she was a Lady of the Bedchamber in which she sends my mother cheques to buy clothes. I had no idea this had happened, and I certainly didn't expect or receive anything from Princess Margaret. When I became Lady-in-Waiting, I had to buy a whole wardrobe of new clothes, all at my own expense. When we were on an official trip abroad, I did receive a small allowance from the Foreign Office, at whose behest we were travelling, but it was only enough for a new pair of shoes or a hat. Life with the Royal family even these days does require a large wardrobe, at Balmoral or Sandringham three changes of outfit are needed every day: daywear, then tea dress and finally an evening dress for dinner.

I still have a lot of my clothes from that time, and of course my two most treasured dresses are my wedding dress and the dress I wore to the late Queen's coronation. Both are exquisite and both designed by Norman Hartnell.

Conversation

I do worry that conversation is a dying art and that humans will lose the ability to connect. It really depresses me when I go out to a restaurant and see a couple not talking but sitting opposite each other on their devices. And I strongly believe phones should be banned and locked away when children get to school. When my children and grandchildren come to stay, we always have proper meals and phones are put away. I make sure we do lots of fun things. We put on little plays and I've still got lots of good dressing-up clothes in a cupboard which they enjoy, and we play various games both inside and outside in the garden, and on the beach. They soon forget about their phones and don't even ask where they are.

I was brought up with very formal meals at Holkham. My mother used to say, 'Anne, you are sitting next to so and so,' and would tell me a little bit about what they did or where they lived so I had something to say to them. She would instruct me to 'engage in conversation, Anne' which I did. I was also sent to a finishing school where we were taught subjects intended to enhance our general knowledge in order that we become interesting conversationalists.

I think the key to being a good conversationalist is to be prepared and to ask lots of questions; be interested in the person you are talking to. It's simple really. It was an immensely useful skill while I was with Princess Margaret when I would end up sitting next to all sorts of people. When we went to Swaziland, I made sure I read up on the country before we went and I ended up sitting next to King Sobhuza and was able to have a very interesting conversation with him. Well, I found it interesting, I'm not sure he did, but I felt I'd done my bit.

It was also true that in my role following on behind Princess Margaret I would notice and pick up on lots of things that would feed into interesting chat later. Similarly with Colin, I was pretty invisible and would soak up situations and be on hand to smooth the way. But now I really have to make an effort not to talk about myself! I've spent a lifetime encouraging other people's conversations and being interested in them, and now for the first time people seem genuinely interested in what I have to say, and I must admit it's rather nice.

Cow

Amy and May's christening was held when we were living in Tite Street, Chelsea in 1971. It was quite a smart affair as Princess Margaret was May's godmother, and one of Amy's godfathers was Hugo Money-Coutts who had helped Colin to develop Mustique. We were all gathering at the house before going over to the Catholic chapel in the grounds of the Royal Hospital, as the main chapel was closed for renovation, when Hugo rang the doorbell. He looked frightfully pleased with himself and said, 'I've bought Amy's present, come and see.' So I stepped outside and there in the middle of Tite Street was a rather large black-and-white cow. I nearly died. I was all dressed up and Princess Margaret was about to arrive. 'How marvellous, Hugo, but what are we going to do with it, we can't leave the cow in the street?' Colin, who'd come rushing out, adored the whole drama of it and rang someone in the Royal Hospital to explain the situation and ask whether it might be possible to tether the cow in the hospital gardens. Luckily for us they agreed, and we took the cow through the gate by our house into the gardens and tied it up there for a couple of days whilst we arranged for someone to transport it up to Glen. In the end this somewhat eccentric present was rather a success as the cow produced two calves which were sold and Amy made a rather nice sum of money from them.

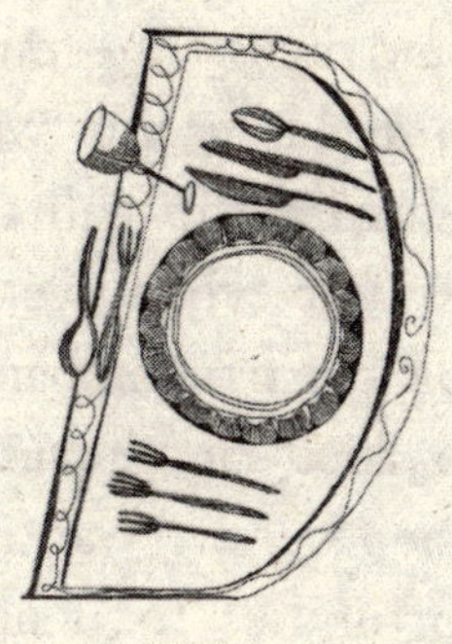

Dancing

There's nothing like dancing to lift the spirits, I've always loved it. I used to love watching *Strictly Come Dancing* but now I find the parts when they talk about their week go on for far too long, I wish there was just more of the dancing.

I remember when we were in Scotland during the war, a dancing teacher would come from Kirriemuir to teach my cousin, my sister and me how to dance the Eightsome Reel and the Sword dance, which is a traditional Scottish Highland dance. We used to skip around in the dining room and loved every second of it. It stood me in good stead with the basics later when during my coming out season we used to go to Scotland in the autumn and were invited to Highland balls. The dances were much more complicated, and a teacher would come to the house the night before the ball to teach you the steps. Many years later when we were at Glen in Scotland we had a permanent band, the Incredible String Band who lived on the estate and used to come and play whenever we wanted them to, so we had endless opportunities to dance, whether after dinner or at picnics.

During the war my mother used to throw parties and dinners for the American officers stationed at the aerodromes in Norfolk and we were asked back when they had the big bands over from America. They taught my sister and me how to jitterbug. We were swung through legs and thrown in the air, it was all tremendous fun, and such a release at a time when my father was rather strict and fussy. Later on, Colin and I used to go to nightclubs and dance to the music of the Rolling Stones, only to dance with Mick Jagger himself at parties on Mustique in later years. There was also a lovely steel band on Mustique which played at parties in people's houses and sometimes at Basil's bar. Princess Margaret used to love the steel bands, and we would quite often be dancing until the small hours of the morning, blissfully away from the prying eyes of any camera lenses.

The Queen and Princess Margaret also enjoyed American line dancing which we used to do at

Sandringham. It was either line dancing or Scottish country dancing at the Royal Palaces – jiving would not have been appropriate.

Diana

I had known Princess Diana for years as she used to live on the Sandringham Estate and attended a nursery school run by my sister Carey at Holkham. Diana's grandmother, Ruth Roche, Baroness Fermoy, was a musician and played the piano beautifully. She was a great friend of my grandfather and started a music festival at King's Lynn with him. I think she realised the tremendous opportunities of renting a house on the Sandringham Estate, eventually becoming Woman of the Bedchamber to Queen Elizabeth, the Queen Mother, to whom she was very close. Her daughter Frances married Johnny Althorp who I had previously been engaged to and thought I was in love with. When I heard about their engagement it was like a dagger to the heart; I felt very down and sad as I was still in love with him. I wasn't invited to their very grand wedding at Westminster Abbey which the Queen and other members of the Royal Family attended as Johnny had been equerry to the King. On reflection I may have had a lucky escape as he did not treat Frances kindly and they eventually divorced. At the time, divorce was considered to be completely socially unacceptable, and Frances' mother Baroness Fermoy testified against her daughter in custody proceedings, which meant that Johnny gained custody of their children. So, he used to turn up at my sister's nursery with Diana each morning clasping her packed lunch and spare shoes in a little case. Carey did say that Diana had a rather tenuous grasp on the truth, and I wonder whether it was the result of being brought up in such an unhappy household.

I knew that Diana was looking for a nanny when she was pregnant with William, and Princess Margaret suggested she employ our wonderful Barbara Barnes as the twins were old enough not to need her. Barbara went for the interview but then didn't hear anything back as to whether she had got the job. It fell to me to follow up with Diana's household, and when I called, I was told, 'Oh yes she's got the job,' although no one had bothered to let Barbara know. Not long afterwards I received a letter from Diana to say how happy and thrilled they were to have Barbara, and inviting Amy and May over to visit and see Barbara in her new surroundings as she knew 'the agony of losing someone like Barbara'. It was very kind of her to make that offer and Amy and May went to Kensington Palace several times to see Barbara and to help bath William and Harry.

I was also extremely touched by the letter she wrote to me after Henry died. She had met him when she was visiting patients suffering from AIDS at St Mary's Paddington and writes of how much it meant to her to have met him and how her visit there was delayed by wanting to spend more time talking to him. She says she was very struck by Henry's inner strength and emphasised how much he had given her the morning she met him in terms of a greater understanding of how to cope with the disease. At a time when most people couldn't even talk about AIDS her directness about the illness and appreciation of Henry was very comforting and it meant a great deal to me.

I do slightly feel that the Queen could have worked harder to try and find Charles a suitable wife. The queens of Greece and Spain used to entertain royal princesses from other European countries in order to find a wife for their sons, but I think because the Queen had fallen in love and had such a successful marriage to Prince Philip she wasn't really focused on Charles in the same way. The Queen Mother and Lady Fermoy at the time were keen that the marriage to Diana should happen. I have a letter the Queen Mother wrote to my mother expressing her delight at the proposed marriage. Prince Philip was also very much in favour of the union, and of course Charles needed to marry a virgin which Diana appeared to be. A friend of mine was at the party where Diana sat next to Charles on a hay bale and was terribly sympathetic to him following the death of Lord

Mountbatten, and although he was there with a girlfriend at the time, she clearly made an impression on him. She was so young when they married, more a friend of Andrew's really, and had had very little life experience. And I think when she became so incredibly popular with the public it was very hard for Prince Charles.

I was invited up to Edinburgh in December 1992 to accompany Princess Margaret at a reception on board the Royal Yacht *Britannia* during the summit marking the end of the British Presidency of the European Council. It was just two days after the announcement of the separation of Prince Charles and Princess Diana and for some reason, probably because she had such star power, Diana had also been invited up to Scotland to be present at the event. It was rather an awkward situation. Princess Margaret told me that Diana was not bringing a lady-in-waiting and asked that I go to see if there was anything she needed. I spent much of the reception talking to Princess Diana, who appeared to be calm and composed but she told me later how grateful she was that I was there and how anxious she had been about the whole event.

Diet

I've always eaten well and been quite careful about what I consume, although I do love offal, and liver is my absolute favourite. In general, I've never really had to diet, and during the war we all had very nice figures, partly because there was so little to eat, and no sugar. However, I did put on weight when I attended Powderham Castle which was my first finishing school where I had been learning how to run a stately home. We spent two weeks with the butler, two weeks with the cook, two weeks with the housekeeper and two weeks with the nanny to learn what needed to be done to run a big house. The Castle had its own farm and we ate extremely well whilst we were there. When I arrived back home, shortly before my coming out dance my mother was horrified. 'I hardly recognise you, you've put on so much weight, you must take it off or no one will even look at you!' So I did, we did what we were told in those days. I found an advert for this silver diet pill which I ordered, and the weight simply fell off. I was thrilled. The pills were quite large and were advertised as having a worm in them, but whatever it was they were very effective, and I lost all the weight I'd put on.

These days you have to be careful not to offend people who are overweight, and I do think it is difficult for working women who are juggling work and family to cook nutritious meals and avoid all the over-processed stuff, there is so much cheap food around. I had to exert a bit of willpower to get my weight down, but these days of course some people can turn to weight-loss injections for help. I suspect I would have used them if they'd been available when I was young.

Dinners

I don't eat dinner, I find I feel much better having just two meals a day and I don't put on weight. However, in the past when I was married, we used to have dinner either in or out with friends every night. We had cooks, of course, so we weren't having to do the cooking ourselves. One great tip, which was something both Princess Margaret and I used to do, was to keep a book in which we wrote down who had been for dinner and what you had given them to eat. It was very useful to make sure that when they came back you didn't give them the same thing. And there was an etiquette to the seating plan in that, as the host, you sat the most important person on your right, and you would spend the first course talking to that person and then the minute the main course was taken away you switched and talked to the person on your left. It meant no one was left out and you had a chance to get to know people on both sides of you. It is still how dinners are run at Sandringham although the King likes to talk to the person on his right for two courses before switching, so I love it when I am seated on his right and tell him, 'I'm so pleased to be sitting on your right so I get you for the first two courses.'

Diplomacy

I think I probably learnt diplomacy at a very young age. My mother threw house parties at Holkham, and we were immediately expected to be on best behaviour and try to help to make people feel at their ease. I would often find guests wandering around the house, quite lost, and then chat to them as I showed them the way to the dining room or drawing room. I was expected to be able to make conversation and help them to feel comfortable.

As a lady-in-waiting, you are really a go-between and must be diplomatic. Princess Margaret used to loathe the unexpected so I soon learnt, if we were going away to a house party for the weekend, to call up in advance and find out what plans were in place, and who she might be sitting next to at dinner. I might gently suggest to the hostess that perhaps sitting Ma'am next to the bishop when she was supposed to be off duty at the weekend might not be the best idea. Often people used to ring me up and ask what colour Princess Margaret was going to wear because they wanted to give her flowers that would complement her outfit, or what she ate, what she drank etc.

I tried to make things as easy as possible for her and for the people who were longing to talk to her but were often quite shy. I have noticed that the moment a member of the Royal Family comes into a room, everybody sort of freezes and often forgets what they wanted to say. I would come along behind and say to them, 'I saw you were having a conversation with Princess Margaret, what did you talk about?' And invariably they would admit they had failed to say exactly what they had wanted to, so I would say, 'Do tell me and I will pass it all on later.' Hopefully making them feel less frustrated that they had missed their opportunity.

I felt sorry for those around President Biden in the run up to the American election when it became obvious that he was not well. It reminded me of the times when I visited President Reagan with Princess Margaret when he clearly was in the early stages of Alzheimer's and mistook me for her. I don't look anything like her, and it was incredibly awkward and tricky to manage without hurting anyone's feelings.

When I was out with Princess Margaret we would often talk beforehand about how she wanted to manage an event, who she may or may not want to talk to and when she might want to be tactfully rescued from a certain situation. I was on the lookout the whole time for things that might go wrong or when it was time to move her on. At dinners or lunches, I usually sat at a table within eye contact to her and if I got the look I could tell she needed me to go over and rescue her.

Sometimes the need for diplomacy could have international implications and when we travelled abroad, we were given notes by the Foreign Office about what not to say to avoid any difficult incident. This was particularly the case when I accompanied Princess Margaret on a visit to Australia in 1975. The country was in the middle of a constitutional crisis, with the opposition blocking the passage of bills to finance the government's agenda. There was a distinct possibility that the government might fall whilst we were there, and I remember Nigel Napier, her private secretary, and other advisors in endless huddles working out what the implications of this might be. We were given lines to take and issues to avoid in the event that the government fell, in which case we might have had to have left Australia early. Happily for us it was ten days after we'd left the country when the Prime Minister was finally dismissed, and the most challenging moment on the trip was persuading Princess Margaret to don sensible shoes for a photocall on Bondi beach.

At other times a breach of diplomacy seemed like the tactful thing to do. On one occasion I was rung up by Princess Margaret's private secretary who said, 'I'm going to ask you if you can do something, but you must keep it under wraps.' I agreed of course and he told me that Princess Margaret was going to visit her uncle, the Duke of Windsor, and his wife who were living in a house just outside Paris. It had to be kept secret as the Queen Mother would not have wanted Princess Margaret to go. She hated the Windsors, partly because she knew the Duchess of Windsor mocked her, and partly because she blamed them for her husband having to become king and then becoming ill and dying prematurely. But Princess Margaret wanted to visit so we did a day trip. We flew to Paris and were met by a car which took us to their house. On the way I asked Princess Margaret what I should do about curtsying – the Duchess of Windsor was never given the HRH title which meant that one didn't have to curtsy to her. But we knew that the Duke minded very much that the Duchess had never been given the title so I wondered whether it might just be polite to curtsy to her. Princess Margaret waited a moment and then said, 'Oh why not?' and so I did. I didn't give a deep curtsy, just a little bob, but I felt it was the right thing to do. That was a moment when strict etiquette was at odds with the needs of tact and diplomacy and I felt we made the right decision.

Driving

I absolutely love driving. I took my test the moment I was seventeen in King's Lynn during market day. I stalled in a herd of cows, but it didn't seem to matter, and I passed. When my mother made me a travelling salesman for Holkham Pottery I used to drive all over the country, including up to Scotland in her Mini-Minor, with my suitcase full of pottery samples. I think I inherited my love of speed from my mother who used to buzz round the Norfolk lanes on her Harley-Davidson motorbike, dressed head to toe in black leather. She really taught me how to drive properly. I never rode a motorbike, but I think we both appreciated the escape driving provided. When I married Colin and realised how demanding he was, driving gave me some reprieve and time to myself. It was before mobile phones so he couldn't get hold of me. I'd put a cassette of opera into the car's tape player and just drive, it was utter bliss.

Colin had some very extravagant cars including a Thunderbird and his father's Rolls Royce. He drove extremely badly so that in the end the safest option was for me to drive him around. At one point I think he got so many points he couldn't drive so that made life simple. I just had little run-around cars during that time, nothing grand, they were much easier to park. Sadly, now I find driving in London impossible with all those twenty mile an hour speed limits and the endless traffic, so I've given up driving there, but I still very much enjoy driving in Norfolk or up to Scotland. Driving has been one of my great pleasures in life.

Dying

As I'm ninety-three I do think about dying quite a bit. Apart from anything else there seem to be endless adverts on television saying one ought to think about various packages to budget for if one wants to be cremated or buried, so it's hard to avoid. I've been slightly putting it off, but I am going to get down to it and tell the children exactly what I want for my funeral service, which will be at my local church here in Burnham Thorpe. It's Nelson's church and I've worshipped here for nearly fifty years. I want to be cremated and I'm going to give very precise instructions about where my ashes are to be scattered. I want them to be divided, and for some of me to buried with my parents in the churchyard at Holkham and the rest to be scattered where my darling Henry was scattered on the Green Hill at Glen. Look out children — it's going to be a bit of a marathon exercise! When my father died his coffin was put in the chapel at Holkham for people from the estate to come and pay their respects before he was buried, but my mother's funeral was at the church here in

Burnham Thorpe where she lived, before she was buried alongside my father.

Some people find it difficult to talk about dying but I actually talk about it quite a lot and the children are quite used to me explaining what I want to happen to all my things when I'm no longer here. They know I've made lists of bequests, sadly many of my friends on the list have now died, so I cross them off one by one. But I think it's very important to be clear about who gets what so that there is no quarrelling when I'm gone. Of course, people do mind about what they inherit, and I had some issues with my sister when my mother died, but I think clarity helps to avoid conflict.

Sadly, I've lost so many of my friends that I spend quite a bit of time at funerals. Some older people I know rather enjoy going to them because it's the only sort of entertainment they get at a time when they aren't asked to many parties. The wake with food and drink afterwards and people to chat to is a nice way to pass the time if you are living on your own. There's a skill to getting the seat you want in the church. Colin's great aunt Margot Asquith, when she went to a funeral or a wedding, would immediately walk straight to the front pew and kneel to pray so that it was impossible to move her and she'd have a prime seat. I always rather prefer sitting at the back.

I am not a fan of memorials which seem to be

increasingly popular. In the past they were only given for very well-known people, public figures, which I think is appropriate, but nowadays lots of people appear to be having a family funeral and then a memorial which goes on forever. My friends and I think they are a bit unnecessary.

I was rather gung-ho about dying until I fractured my back and was in the most appalling pain. I've never experienced pain like it, and it did make me have great sympathy for those who believe in assisted dying. I had always thought it was quite a dangerous road to go down and it conflicts with my religious faith, but my experience of terrible pain was sobering and has given me pause for thought about the whole issue.

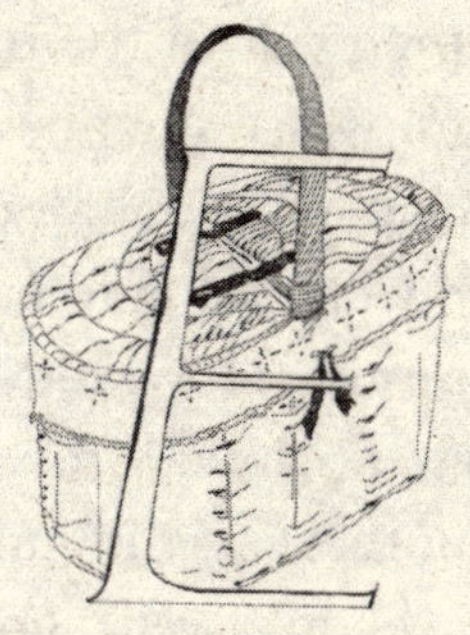

Eels

When he was a boy Prince Charles used to come over to Holkham quite often and my father taught him to fish for eel on the lake. The eel were caught using a long wooden trap which was green at one end and red on the other and which were left, a bit like lobster pots, in the water. He used to row out with Prince Charles onto the lake and if the trap had flipped upside down so that the red end was showing it meant that an eel had been caught inside. My father asked Charles whether he had ever eaten eel and when he confessed he hadn't, my father marched him to the kitchen to cook what they had caught. The problem was that the nerves of the eel remain intact even after they were cut and so bits of eel started jumping out of the frying pan all over the kitchen floor. I was remembering this recently with the (now) King who confessed to me, 'When your father said we were going to eat them I thought I was going to be sick.' However, with immaculate manners as always, I came across a letter he had written to my mother at the time in which he politely says 'the eel was very good, especially in butter'. Rather amusingly he also thanks my mother for letting him drive her van and her Jag round the estate; he was twelve at the time!

Entertaining

I've done a great deal of entertaining in my life. Even when I was a child at Holkham my mother was often away because she was Lady of the Bedchamber to the Queen, so I used to take her place if my father had dinner parties. We were always taught, even as children, to look people in the eye and try to think of interesting things to say. Sometimes my father would have shooting parties which although arranged by my mother, she was not invited to attend as they were all male affairs. We were in fact rather pleased when this happened as we were allowed to go off and watch television which was a real treat.

When I married Colin, he loved entertaining and in addition to giving a lot of dinner parties in London we also had house parties when we were in Scotland at Glen in the summer. I think the most people I ever had at the house were thirty-six; we had a huge photograph taken of everyone outside. It was a bit like running a hotel. First there was breakfast in bed; all married women had breakfast in bed. Unmarried women didn't wear tiaras or have breakfast in bed.

They had their own table by the window in the dining room, while the men sat at a separate table eating a substantial breakfast of porridge, kippers, eggs and sausage, and reading their newspapers or talking about shooting. I used to love going to the pantry the night before to see all the breakfast trays laid out for the married women with beautiful tray cloths, a small teapot or coffee jug, egg cup, cereal bowl, napkin, the whole thing looked so pretty. You would always be asked when you arrived what you would like to have for breakfast. This happened when I was at home as well – I always had breakfast in bed separately from Colin.

When entertaining there were various details that were important to consider. Sheets always had to be linen, and the pillows would have an embroidered frill but never embroidery on the pillow itself which would be uncomfortable to lie on. And there were generally two big square pillows on each side of a double bed, never long, always square. We also used to have two hot-water bottles in a double bed, one on each side, in immaculately ironed linen covers. Some men didn't like them, Colin used to fling his onto the floor but some of the houses we visited were freezing and they were useful. The maids used to come in to turn down the bed and put a side light on whilst we were at dinner. The hot-water bottles weren't put in until later as we never went to bed before midnight. Woe betide finding petals or a chocolate on the bed – that would have been considered terribly common!

We used to put two types of loo paper in the bathrooms. We would fan out sheets of bronco, the very shiny, hard paper – my father was a stickler for bronco – and we would secure them with an attractive large crystal or a shell on top so that you could just pull out a piece at a time. However, bronco loo paper really didn't do the job, so there was also nice soft paper available. We also used to put headed writing paper on every desk in the bedrooms; some people had little line drawings of the house on their writing paper and postcards of the house. You didn't put out too much stationery, however, as you knew it would all be taken.

In the evening if we were at Glen, I would oversee the laying of the dinner table to make sure it was done properly. We didn't have a full-time old-fashioned butler but used to hire one in the summer and they varied, some were very good, but some weren't, so I always needed to check. I would do the place à table and write out people's names on cards, so everyone knew where to sit.

The job of a hostess is to make everyone feel comfortable. You need to keep an eye open to see if anyone is being left out and, if so, bring somebody else up to them and stimulate conversation. It's also so important to notice if one of the guests is spending ages before dinner talking to another guest who you know they are about to sit next to at the table, as in that case you need to whisk one of them away. At Glen during the daytime, I loved going for long walks and would ask 'Anybody else like to go for a walk?' and we'd go up to the loch and sit there and chat, or I'd arrange for people to play tennis or croquet. There could be challenging guests. I think the most extraordinary was Raine Spencer, who became Princess Diana's stepmother. She arrived and said she would like somebody to unpack for her, which was often done, but to my astonishment when I was walking down the corridor, I heard a ghastly banging noise coming from her bedroom. I went down to ask the housekeeper what was going on and she said, 'Oh Lady Spencer said that the rail in the cupboard for her dresses wasn't high enough and so she asked the house carpenter to come and raise it, but I thought she'd asked you?' Of course she hadn't, I had no idea. Princess Margaret was by far the easiest guest, she always brought her own maid, so I really didn't have to do anything for her.

Expeditions

Colin was very restless, he always needed to be doing something and that was particularly the case when he came to Norfolk where there was really only room for us and Princess Margaret, and possibly one other couple to stay. So I used to organise expeditions to lovely houses in Norfolk. Christopher Tadgell, a friend who is an architectural historian, used to suggest rather unusual smaller houses to visit that often weren't open to the public. I fear I used to rather horrify people when I'd ring up out of the blue and ask whether we could possibly come and look at their house with Princess Margaret. But I was always quick to say that they mustn't worry about entertaining us, and that we would bring our own picnic if there was somewhere in their garden we could put down a rug. Drinks were very important. Princess Margaret liked a gin and tonic at lunchtime, whisky in the evening.

Trips to the beach were also very popular with Princess Margaret and we live close to the sea. When we were younger, we used to run together into the water but after she'd been to the Caribbean she quite naturally found the North Sea a bit chilly. We'd go for walks or picnic on the beach when the weather was warm enough.

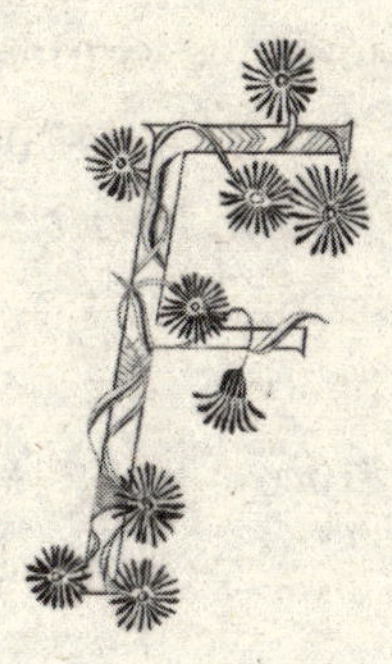

Flowers

I was taught flower arranging as part of my preparation for running a stately home at Powderham Castle and I really enjoyed it. I've always been interested in and loved flowers. I've been to Covent Garden flower market a couple of times, which was magical, seas of flowers with a wonderful smell in the air.

An important part of preparing to entertain guests was organising the flowers for the house. Glen was a big house with high ceilings, so you needed to have quite large arrangements. I had a great friend called Sarah Henderson who used to come up before a house party to help me with the flowers. We would decide in advance, with the help of the gardener, which types of blooms we wanted to use from our picking border. All big houses had a flower room with everything you might need in it, like vases, secateurs, wire and string. The flowers we had chosen would be laid out by type on a huge table or on a big sheet on the floor, along with the greenery required. A flower boy would be on hand to lift down the large vases we needed, and we would arrange the stems in the vase. In addition to the large arrangements every bedroom would have fresh flowers on the dressing table and in the bathroom. There is nothing more welcoming than flowers in the bathroom. I quickly learned how important it is to make sure vases are washed properly and disinfected after each use or the fresh flowers won't last any time at all.

One of my great joys in life now is to go round my garden really looking at the flowers, at how intricate and beautiful they are. I might pick some lilac or other flower that is in bloom in the garden to offer to the church if there's a wedding or a funeral happening there.

Flying

Flying used to be so glamorous. I remember the first flight I ever went on was on a Boeing Stratocruiser to America in 1951. There were proper bunk beds with sheets and little curtains you could pull round for privacy. I had the top bunk, and it was wonderful. No flight since has lived up to that one although I did fly very comfortably when I was accompanying Princess Margaret. I remember when I was flying with her to Australia the aeroplane had a bar upstairs and you could go up from first class and sit and have breakfast and dinner; it was great. She was not a nervous flyer. There was a time when we were flying to America and we hit the most awful thunderstorm. I was clutching onto my seat and she looked at me and patted my hand and said, 'Don't worry, Anne, we'll either die or we'll live and that's that, no point worrying about it, but I think perhaps we ought to have another drink.'

Friendship

Friendship is very important to me, and I think there is something about friendship from childhood which is particularly special. You speak the same language, it's easy and you understand each other. Some of the friends I made at boarding school have stayed friends throughout my life. The thing about real friends is that you don't need to have too many of them, I think six to eight is the perfect number. And they don't have to be the same sex, one of my really good friends is male and I can talk to him about anything. I have also been so lucky to have made younger friends as well, which is particularly important when you get to my age. Every year a Turkish friend invites me on holiday and he has some much younger friends, and in turn they've become friends of mine which is lovely.

I was at an event the other day talking about domestic abuse when a man in the audience said, 'I've been abused in my relationship and I feel so sad and hopeless, do you have any advice?' And my advice to him was to talk to his friends, not to be shy or embarrassed about it, domestic abuse is nothing to be ashamed of and once you talk to people the problem, whatever it is, feels minimised. Sometimes talking to friends won't work or be sufficient, and you need to find professional help, but for me one of the great things about friendship, is having people you can really talk to.

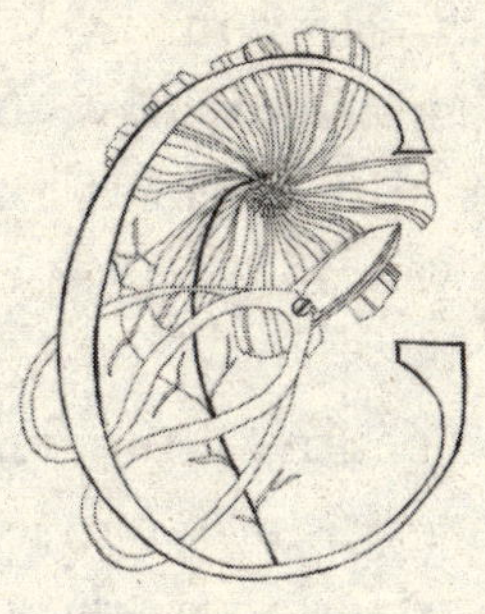

Games

I vividly remember the first game I played when we were in Scotland during the war. Our wonderful nanny, Billy Williams, used to play a game called the Dark Game, which was like murder in the dark. I remember being in the nursery and Billy turning all the lights out and trying to catch us. It was utterly thrilling, crawling under tables and chairs and trying to escape. Of course, in the end she caught us all and that was that, but I still remember the excitement of it.

We have always played lots of games, ones that are suitable for the house you are in at the time. Glen was perfect for hide and seek and kick the can, lots of winding staircases, odd passages and nooks and crannies to hide in. Now in my small London flat when I have the grandchildren, we might play racing demon or another card or board game. It's lovely to have games that we can all play together, I think they really enjoy it.

I'm terribly competitive I'm afraid. It used to be quite tricky when I was playing racing demon with Princess Margaret trying to work out whether to let her win or jolly well beat her. I used to alternate. She used to look at me sometimes and say, 'Anne are you trying to win or are you letting me?'

Colin was also very competitive, and I regularly used to let him win so that he didn't have a tantrum, he was not a good loser. I've played bridge all my life, but Colin was the worst person to play with. Once when we were staying with friends he tipped up the table and stormed out. After that I did say to him, 'Look, Colin, I really think we can't play together. I think I probably irritate you and I'm terrified you are going to tip the table over again.' From that moment on we didn't play together, and I really enjoyed bridge after that.

Gardening

I'm a housemaid in the garden because what I really like doing is weeding and a bit of pruning and snipping. I don't know a great deal about plants; I like them and the more ordinary ones I know but I'm not a proper gardener. However, I love my garden and enjoy my 'housemaiding' around it. It gives me great joy to haul out weeds and make it all look neat and tidy.

I also love going to look round other peoples' gardens, although sometimes it can be a bit depressing as you know that your own is never going to look as good. I love the walled garden at Houghton and the Duke of Buccleuch's garden at Boughton is wonderful. The King has also shown me round his garden at Highgrove which is fantastic. He's a very keen gardener and is currently redoing the gardens at Sandringham, which I'm sure will be amazing.

Princess Margaret used to take us to the Chelsea Flower Show as one of the 'treats' she put on for her friends and staff, but these days I just enjoy watching it on the television. It's so interesting the way gardens have changed. Now they are all wild-flowers, rocks, gravel, desert gardens and water that is recycled every hour. I suppose it's right that the gardens are adapted to cope with climate change. Fashions change in gardening as in everything else, but I'm afraid I still love a neatly mown lawn.

Getting On With It

I've talked a great deal about my stiff upper lip, and my mother was like that, very much so; that you just got on with things, you didn't complain. I hate people who complain. However bad you are feeling, the minute you start thinking in a positive way it really does help a lot. In the past I've always just tried to get on with things, but I did notice when I fractured my back that one is inclined to feel sorry for oneself and feel as though you can't do things. Once I had got over the really agonising part, I thought I needed to pull myself together: 'Out you go, get dressed, carry on.' So I did, whilst knowing that if it was impossible I could just lie down or sit for a moment and that has helped.

I think people of my generation are much tougher than young people today. I think it could be because when there was a war on everybody had to work together and young people had an objective. It was about doing something for the greater good, whether we were made to sign up or do other things to help the war effort. Today there's much less of a sense of collective endeavour, the young seem to be much more focused on themselves, although I do realise many have different and difficult things to deal with so it's hard to generalise.

In my very worst moments when I was in hospital with Christopher after his accident, knowing that my other two boys were going to die, every now and then my sister or cousin would come and sit with him, and I would escape to Norfolk. I would take out my little Mirror dinghy and sail out to sea. It's only a tiny boat, but with two sails and a centreboard to deal with there was a lot to think about. It distracted me and took me away from everything and for a moment I could relax. Gardening is something else which I found served a similar purpose, weeding and planting and being outside.

The great thing I say to people who are going through a really, really difficult time is 'love yourself, look after yourself.' Maybe have one treat a day, whether you watch your favourite film or take yourself off for a walk. It's not self-indulgent, it's necessary. If you think you are doing something badly, or you're not coping 'properly' it's easy to hate yourself and it shows, it just makes you even more miserable and angry. But if you say to yourself 'I am trying, I'm doing a good job', it helps. For me I felt so lucky to have had my boys for so many years and to have been able to look after them, and talk to them when they were ill, that was some kind of comfort, and of course I had wonderful friends supporting me.

Hair

I've been extremely lucky all my life with my hair. I'm ninety-three and I've never had a grey hair or had to dye it. When I was in Mustique, I used to put lemon juice on it to encourage the sun streaks. It's also thick and easy to manage so when I'd been swimming, I'd just wash it in the shower and let it dry in the sun, especially in the early days when there was no electricity. I do think hair matters to people and having a good cut is so important, especially when you get older, as the old face needs a bit of help. I never used to visit the hairdresser's much except when I was on a trip with Princess Margaret. She travelled with a hairdresser, so we'd have a blow-dry every morning, which was heaven.

There was one terrible moment in the early 1950s when my grandmother sent me to the hairdresser's for a perm. It was a frightfully grand hairdresser's on Sloane Street and I was whirled in and attached to a machine which permed my hair. I left with my perfectly nice straight hair tightly curled, looking like a sheep. Never again!

Handrails

Must not be used unless absolutely necessary! I think it's so important to go up and downstairs without holding on so that you strengthen your core and sharpen your sense of balance. I rented out my house in Norfolk once and the person who took it had a disabled wife, so he installed handrails all over the house. When I moved back in, I removed them all, apart from one in the downstairs loo, and to my amazement I found it was actually quite useful after I'd broken my back. But I've weaned myself off it, and handrails are out again.

Hats

I've always loved hats; my generation always wore a hat of one description or another. I still wear a beret when I go to church, I would feel very odd without one as when I was younger we would always wear a hat and gloves to church. It was also the greatest treat to buy a beautiful new hat to go to Ascot or to a Buckingham Palace garden party. When I was accompanying Princess Margaret as Lady-in-Waiting, I always wore a hat. Freddie Fox was the milliner she and other members of the Royal Family tended to favour, as well as Philip Treacy. I'm lucky enough to still have most of my hats, a huge array of them in hat boxes at home. One of the wonderful things about living in North Norfolk is that I'm quite close to the most amazing hat shop in Burnham Market. Burnham Hats I think must have more headwear than any other shop, apparently they have over seventy thousand hats, organised into rooms of different colours. I bought my hat for Prince William's wedding there; it was a joy to go in and choose one. Mine was a pink and cream straw hat which matched my dress.

Hotels

I used to adore staying in hotels. My son Charlie said he would have liked to live in a hotel, he thought that room service was wonderful and I must admit I find it hard to resist. My favourite hotel is the Ritz in London. When I was having my second child Henry, who ended up being nearly eleven pounds, I was exhausted and could hardly move. When I was nearing the end of my pregnancy Colin very sweetly said, 'We're moving to the Ritz until the baby comes.' It was such a treat – magical old-fashioned luxury and I loved every minute. I was rather sad I only had two days there before Henry arrived.

I worry these days when I'm staying in a hotel that there will be some very loud person in the room next door making a noise, so I like hotels slightly less than I did. However, the last time I went to Mustique I stayed at the Cotton House, which is the only hotel on the island, and you can stay in private bungalows in the grounds. Tropical birds fly around as you are eating lunch, trying to grab your food so the tables have water pistols on them to keep the birds away, I don't think we ever managed to hit one, but it was great fun trying!

Husbands

I've written so much about Colin in my previous books that I've nothing much to add here other than choose wisely. And very importantly, don't be led down the garden path with protestations of 'once I'm married to you I won't ever lose my temper again'. I'm afraid that simply will not be true. Be aware that any promises made before marriage will most likely be quickly forgotten.

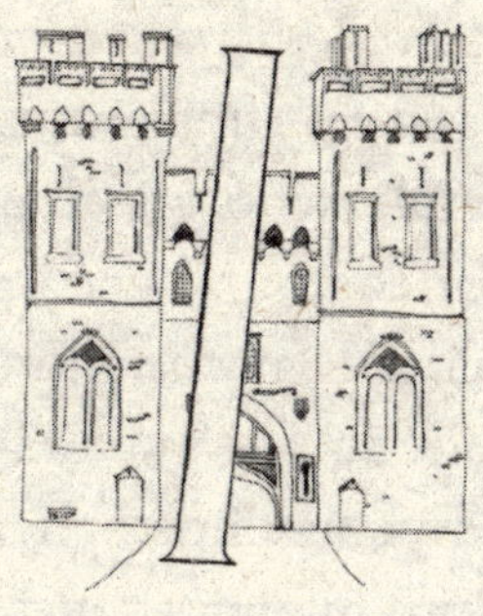

Impatience

I'm afraid impatience is one of my sins. I've probably got lots of sins, but impatience is definitely one of them. I've always been impatient. My grandmother, my mother's mother, was also incredibly impatient, perhaps it's an inherited trait. It particularly comes out when I'm driving. I can't bear getting stuck behind someone who is driving at fifteen miles an hour, in the end I have to whirl past them and you can bet that's the moment a speed camera will get me.

I think I have calmed down in my old age because I used to be terribly impatient if people were slow or didn't understand what I was saying. Quite often probably, it was me not being sufficiently clear, but it still used to drive me mad. It really is a sin though and can lead to trouble as when you are impatient you miss things, and you make mistakes. But when I come across people who are impatient I do have great sympathy for them.

However, the older I get the more I appreciate the things other people do for me and this tempers me somewhat. When my son Christopher had his accident, I had to learn to curb my impatience as it really wasn't productive or in any way helpful to be impatient with him. I had to go slowly and was quite firm, refusing to get him aids like chair lifts to go up and down stairs so that he would learn to manage on his own. I also think he had the same effect on Colin who was wonderful with him and managed to control his temper when Christopher was involved. When Christopher was well enough, Colin took him out to St Lucia and rented a cottage for him in Soufriere where he could live independently. But Colin also paid for two ladies who lived behind the cottage to keep an eye on him. They might follow Christopher when he went out walking so they could scoop him up if he fell over, but he had the sense of living independently. Now he is married to my wonderful daughter-in-law Johanna, for whom I have huge admiration and who looks after him so well.

Inheritance

Aristocratic families in England practise primogeniture, which in most contexts means that girls can't inherit. If you look when you go round some of the larger stately homes in England you may notice that often there aren't many little pretty objects like little boxes lying about on tables; often the daughters of the house who knew they weren't going to be left anything would quietly squirrel away what they could.

I knew at an early age that I wasn't going to inherit Holkham and my younger sister Carey and I just burst into tears when we were told at school that our mother had had a third child who was also a little girl. We knew how frightfully disappointing it would be to my father, especially as my mother had such an awful time giving birth to my younger sister, Sarah, that she was unable to have any more children. It meant that the Estate would have to pass to the wider family, in our case to my father's cousin who remained in South Africa and left the running of the estate to his son Edward who finally inherited in 1976.

On the other hand, in France there is often very little left at all inside the stately homes as everything is divided equally between the children. I think that's rather sad too. At least in England the houses are full of paintings and furniture so there is an integrity to them, as well as interesting things to look at.

Since 2015 the Royal Family has allowed women to inherit the Crown, so it is very sad to me that the aristocracy has not followed suit. In the past I have signed letters to the prime minister, including to Boris Johnson, asking for a bill to be introduced to abolish male primogeniture but I suppose it will never be top of the government's agenda. It's also true that as it is mostly incumbent men who sit in the House of Lords, they are unlikely to be sympathetic to the cause.

Interior Design

We've had a great many houses as Colin loved buying new properties; I slightly lost count of the number of times we moved house. But our main homes were Glen in Scotland, the Great House in Mustique and Hill House in Notting Hill and, of course, the lovely farmhouse in Norfolk where I still live. I was never allowed much say in doing up any of the houses I lived in with Colin. The only room for which I was allowed to make the interior design decisions was my bedroom and I derived a great deal of joy from choosing pretty fabrics, often with the help of Colefax and Fowler. I always had a four-poster bed in my room and found there was something terribly exciting about the smell of new material or a new carpet.

In Mustique we used an interior designer called John Stefanidis who, having been born in Egypt understood hot climates and the ways in which houses needed to be furnished in the heat. He did a lot of houses for Colin, in England as well, and was very good with him, even when Colin insisted on doing up the drawing room at Hill House in London to resemble a railway hotel he'd stayed at in the Midlands. It was pretty quickly redone at great expense. Colin was terribly extravagant and loved India where he met up with a great friend, Mitch Crites, who was a dealer in artefacts. Colin used to go on great trips with Mitch, one time spying an exquisite temple which the maharajas had used as a lunching place on days when they were out hunting tigers. He bought the temple for a small fortune, and then had it shipped back to Mustique in pieces accompanied by eight locals who were supposed to know how to put it up. They really had no idea, and Colin constantly lost his temper with them, eventually enlisting the help of Arnie Hasselqvist, who was a Swedish architect Colin worked with in Mustique, and who managed to piece the whole thing together. It's still there, and when the moon is up people walking along the beach can see its lace-like marble reflected in the light. In a way this delicate temple is Colin's lasting legacy to the island.

I adored our house Glen in Scotland: from the outside it looks a bit like a fairy-tale castle with lots of turrets and gargoyles in a valley surrounded by beautiful hills. When my father-in-law remarried, his new wife, Elizabeth Glenconner, did up the house influenced by an interior designer called Syrie Maugham. She concentrated on making things light and bright and painted the hallway white and laid a beautiful pale green carpet. But she also squared off all the rooms that had rounded corners and put in plain ceilings, in keeping with a trend at the time for all things Georgian. When Colin inherited the house, we wanted to put it back to how it had been and we were delighted to discover the original moulded ceilings, which had been covered up with plain board. The ceilings were in fantastic condition as they had never been repainted, which had happened in other houses, causing them to lose the definition of the moulding. We reincorporated the turreted corners in all the rooms; in the nursery we used one for the toys and one as the nanny's kitchen. I also went to the William Morris Gallery to look at some of the old papers there and had one or two of them reprinted for the rooms at Glen. We kept the light hallway with the green carpet and the overall effect was of a lovely, light, happy house; it was a great success. I would happily have lived at Glen, but Colin was too impatient because, sitting as it did at the head of a valley, Colin said he couldn't live anywhere where there was only one way out.

At quite an early stage in our marriage, realising Colin was extremely unreliable, my father said, 'I think, Anne, you should have a place of your own in case you ever have to live by yourself,' and so he took me to see two farmhouses owned by the Estate that had become redundant as farmhouses. One was on the marsh at Burnham Overy Staithe, and although it was lovely, it was also quite bleak. I had visions of Magwitch coming out over the marsh and was worried about flooding. I opted instead for a house in a village close to Holkham which I totally fell in love with. It had a beautiful walled garden with lots of barns and outbuildings brimming with potential. Colin had absolutely nothing to do with it and so I was finally able to do up a house myself, together with a friend who worked for Colefax and Fowler. They have a wonderful sale once a year where they sell offcuts and I managed to find some beautiful material to make curtains for half price, which was extremely satisfying. Another friend very kindly gave me the present of the time of this marvellous decorator from Colefax and Fowler who used to arrive in his Rolls Royce with the back full of paint pots and brushes and he painted two of my main rooms. My bedroom he painted a divine blue, which is a difficult colour to get right, but he did and it's absolutely perfect. To wash its face I used to rent the house out over the summer and because it's near the sea it was always very popular. But now I'm back living here and just being in the house and garden gives me immense pleasure.

Another very good friend of mine, who memorably took a central role in our all-male production of *Swan Lake* at Glen, was the Hungarian fabric designer Michael Szell. He was thrilled to receive a summons to Buckingham Palace to discuss the redecorating of the Queen's bedroom. He was less thrilled to be told that in fact the Queen preferred Laura Ashley to his more striking designs. All was not lost, however, and he subsequently designed the Throne Room at Windsor Castle as well as receiving a number of other commissions for the Royal Family.

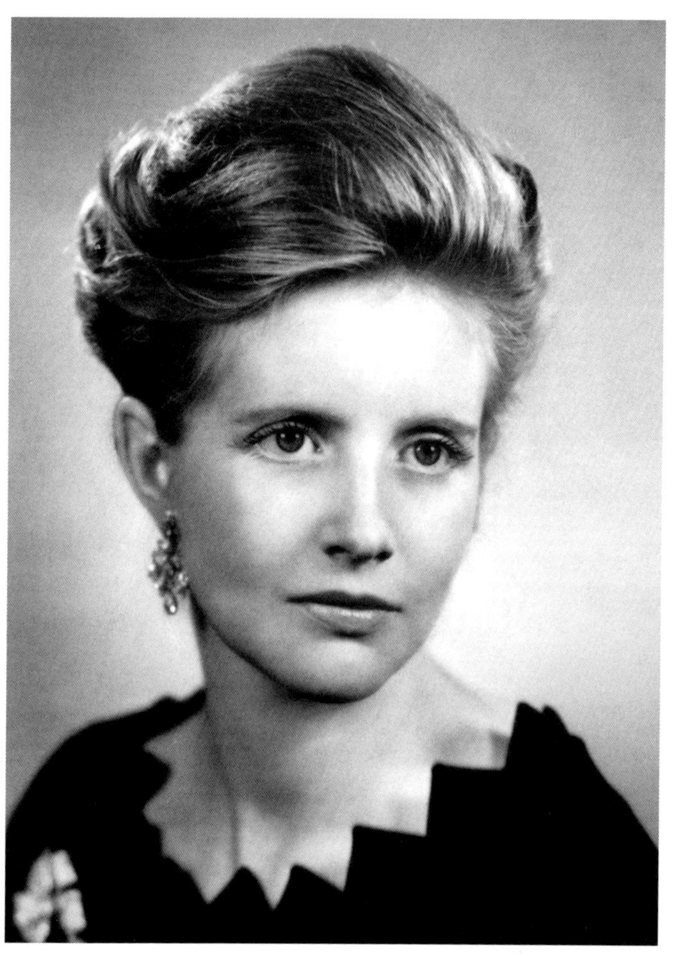

H is for hair – I was pregnant at the time this photograph was taken and it made me feel more glamorous to have my hair up.

A is for Amateur dramatics at Glen, Princess Margaret
dressed as Brunhilde and Mae West

Looking on whilst Princess Margaret played piano
and Colin led the singing after dinner

C is for Charity – With Vera Lynn and Frankie Howard at charity dinners held to raise money for children with cerebral palsy

H is for Hats – with my great friend Ingrid Channon at a party in 1966 thinking we looked wonderful in our hats!

J is for Jewellery – With Jerry Hall at a charity event. I'm wearing my tiara of stars

C is for Cow – Godmothers Princess Margaret holding May, and Diane Nutting holding Amy, at their christening, having just dealt with the cow brought to the front door as a christening present

E is for Eels – clad in his waders, Prince Charles with my mother at Balmoral. My mother appears to be smoking a pipe!

M is for Mustique and B is for Basil's Bar

With Princess Margaret
on Mustique

Bianca and Mick Jagger at
Colin's Golden Ball 1976

Basil Charles of Basil's
Bar with his partner of
12 years, Lady Royston

The Queen at Les
Jolies Eaux, Princess
Margaret's house on
Mustique, with
Oliver Messel who
designed the house
and royal goldsmith
Stuart Devlin

E is for expeditions – Colin and Princess Margaret stroking the
Buddha at Sandringham on one of our expeditions there

With Colin, Roddy and Princess Margaret at my house in
Norfolk before setting out for a picnic

D is for Diana,
Princess of Wales,
behind the wheel
of David Linley's
sports car on a visit
to Balmoral

Corgis in surprisingly benign
mood on the same visit

On board the Royal Yacht
Britannia before the European
Council reception at which I
acted as Lady-in-Waiting to
Princess Diana

J is for Joy – Sailing my Mirror
dinghy and sitting in my
summerhouse looking out
at my garden, both of which
bring me immense joy

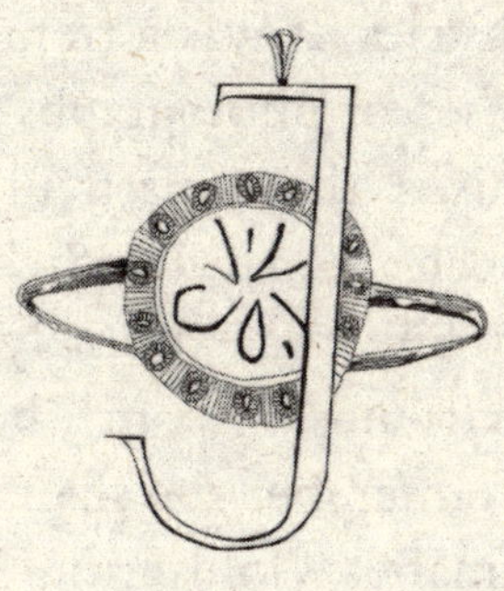

Jealousy

I'm afraid jealousy rears its ugly green head quite often. My poor sister Carey was, I think, rather jealous when I was a Maid of Honour at the Coronation. I was the centre of attention, I was in the press, a part of history, and photographed endlessly, so it must have been hard for her to take. Happily, my father received a letter from Norfolk, Virginia in America about a great azalea fête they were having to celebrate the azalea season there. They needed an Azalea Queen for the fête and wrote to my father to ask for a recommendation for someone from Norfolk in England. He suggested my sister take the role, so she went over to America, complete with her own maids of honour from all the NATO countries. It was a tremendous success. There were masses of photographs of her, and she was much admired there, particularly by lots of handsome American naval officers who were stationed nearby. She was extremely pretty and had many more boyfriends than me, but she was also very naughty. I remember she shared a coming out dance with Annabel Goldsmith, who was then called Annabel Vane-Tempest-Stewart. At one point the Duke of Gloucester said to my mother he'd like to meet them, and my mother looked for the two of them everywhere, but they'd already left and gone to a nightclub.

Jealousy is so hard to deal with especially when you are young. I remember being very jealous of people who spent time with my mother, as having been parted from her for three years during the war I was always desperate be with her. I longed for her to be with me constantly to make up for the time apart and I think that longing coloured my childhood. I remember once when my mother's godson came to stay she gave him one of her cameras. As photography was one of my passions, I could hardly bear it and had to run away to burst into tears. That was pure jealousy and is one of those episodes from childhood that stays with me.

Later on I had to deal with Colin's jealousy around my appointment as Lady-in-Waiting. He adored Princess Margaret and couldn't understand why she'd chosen me to occupy a position that was so close to her. I had to remind him that I had known her far longer than he had, and he just had to get used to it, but Princess Margaret was very understanding and sometimes where he had a connection to the place we were visiting, he used to come with us when we went abroad.

Jewellery

I've always loved jewellery, not that I've ever had that much. I have one or two pieces that I love wearing, an engagement ring that I always wear and a very thin gold wedding band. I think Colin was rather disappointed that I chose it, but the great thing about a thin band is that you have room to wear other rings with it. I wondered whether Colin thought I didn't really want to be married, which to be honest at moments during our honeymoon I rather wished I hadn't been.

Both Princess Margaret and I were very keen on costume jewellery, particular from Kenneth Lane. He was a famous costume jeweller and when he was in London, he would come to Kensington Palace with a whole array of his latest treasures for Princess Margaret to choose from. In a way it's much more relaxing wearing costume jewellery because it's not the end of the world if you lose it. Ken Lane's pieces were so good it was pretty hard to tell whether they were real or not, and if people expect you to be wearing real jewels they think it's genuine even if it's not. When I was travelling with Princess Margaret, we had security with us so I would tend to wear the real thing. Colin bought me some diamond stars which I wore like a tiara, and which could also double-up as brooches. I didn't have a tiara of my own, but my diamond stars were much more flexible. May wore them as a tiara at her wedding and looked beautiful in them.

Jobs

I think it's such a good idea to give children jobs to do around the house. My children were given little tasks, especially if they wanted to earn a bit of pocket money. My father was very keen that we all had jobs during the school holidays. One of mine was to air the Codex Leicester which was a leather-bound notebook of observations and diagrams by Leonardo da Vinci. I would really have preferred to have been given some silver to clean – I used to love the smell of that pink paste you use. However, I did a bit too much silver cleaning when I was at finishing school and now I hate doing it and avoid it like the plague. The job I most enjoyed was polishing the shell of the huge and very old tortoise at Powderham Castle, rather an odd weekly task to be given but I would make it incredibly shiny and found it very satisfying.

Joy

Most of the time one must battle along, coping with the day-to-day business of living but occasionally there are quiet moments of joy and I think it's so important to recognise and appreciate them. Two people who bring me joy daily when I'm in London are Rajendra and Yogesh Rajkotia, who used to own a newsagent near where I live and now sell their papers from a car boot on a side road in Holland Park. Every morning when I go to collect my paper they are ready with a smile and a chat, always so welcoming and friendly it's a really wonderful start to the day. They brighten the morning for the whole neighbourhood.

I can find joy quite unexpectedly whilst walking around my garden and suddenly notice the first flowers on a rose bush that I'm very fond of. Trees to me are also very special. I have a huge and wonderful walnut tree in my garden which is apparently about one hundred and fifty years old. In the summer I often go and sit just looking at it, whilst in the autumn when the walnuts drop it's a race between me and the squirrels to pick up the nuts which I enjoy throughout the winter.

My children and grandchildren bring me great joy, whether it's looking at the sweet face of my new great-granddaughter Miriam in a photo I've just been sent, or listening to a grandchild phoning up to say they've passed an exam or hearing them bubbling with excitement to tell you what a wonderful time they had on holiday. All these moments are important to cling onto and remember.

There are also the more obvious events that spark joy. When my daughter May was getting married, my cousin very kindly said that I could hold her wedding at Holkham. I arranged it in just the same way that my wedding had been organised, and one of the most magical moments was seeing her come down the stairs in her beautiful wedding dress, wearing the star tiara I had also worn. The whole day was wonderful and a memory to be cherished, as was the moment after Queen Elizabeth's coronation when we all came out onto the balcony at Buckingham Palace and saw the huge crowds all cheering and shouting. One could almost physically feel their joy which was incredibly thrilling.

I have memories of quieter moments from my childhood which can elicit the same feelings. My mother occasionally used to take us away from the more formal life at Holkham, where my father was very strict and we had to be absolutely on time for meals and all that sort of thing, to camp in a hut on the beach. It had a balcony and inside there was one big room and a small kitchen. When it got dark, we used to take our nets to go shrimping. As we walked down to the sea it was sparkling with phosphorescence, and I remember thinking it was like magic. In Mustique we used to swim at night when the moon was full but low and you felt as though you could swim towards the moon and almost touch it. I'll never forget those moments.

Jubilee

I remember the Queen asking me, with all the other Maids of Honour from the Coronation, to the celebrations for her Silver Jubilee in June 1977. We were asked to Buckingham Palace where we sat in an extended royal box and watched a concert in the garden. During the interval the Royal Family went inside to have something to eat and we were all given a wonderful picnic basket each. I remember sitting there, eating the most delicious food and drinking champagne whilst watching the performers. Vera Lynn was one of the artists and when she sang 'We'll Meet Again' I noticed one or two people snuffling into their hankies. I think that was the last time the six of us Maids of Honour were all together after the Coronation at a formal event.

Kindness

I think kindness is absolutely essential if one's going to live one's life in any way with joy. It was particularly brought home to me during Covid when people showed tremendous kindness to each other. I live in a village on my own and lovely local people used to leave bread and other gifts of food at my door. One day this darling little girl on a pink tricycle came and rang the bell and then scooted off, leaving a pizza her mother had cooked for me on the doorstep; it was just so thoughtful. It's particularly important at times when people celebrate with their families, to think of those who are living on their own and invite them over. I have a friend who has no other family, and she generally comes over to spend Christmas with us. The more the merrier.

When I was unwell, I became particularly aware of the kindness of others. A friend who lives quite near said to me, 'Just ring up any time if you aren't feeling well or need help, and I can always pop over.' So incredibly kind, and although I haven't needed to do so, it's very reassuring to know that I could. And my daughters and daughter-in-law have really pushed the boat out to be kind, taking it in turns to stay with me until I was better. It's tremendously healing to feel that thoughtfulness, both to give and to receive it.

King

I've known the King since he was three. He used to come and stay at Holkham with his nanny whenever he had one of those childhood ailments like mumps or measles. The Queen hadn't been away to school and had never contracted any of them, so it was important she didn't catch anything from him. He absolutely adored my mother, and we had so many happy times together at Holkham.

The wonderful thing is that now I live very near Sandringham, I'm quite often asked to dinner if he's on his own. Queen Camilla has her own children and grandchildren, and I think that at ninety-three she probably thinks I'm a safe pair of hands to keep him company. They send a car for me, which is really kind as I don't like driving at night, and I go over and have these lovely dinners with him where we just talk and reminisce; it's perfect. Before I knew my back was fractured, I was in a great deal of pain, and when I turned up for dinner, he realised and very kindly rang his own doctor, who spoke to my doctor and between them I managed to get the right treatment. I was so grateful for that.

It was also such a joy to have been at his coronation. A few days after the ceremony he invited me over for dinner so we could talk through the ways in which his coronation had differed from his mother's. There aren't many of us who were at both, and I think he wanted to hear what I had to say. He was just four when his mother was crowned and he says he remembers being really annoyed at having his hair plastered down with some kind of hair cream for the event.

I think he's already moved seamlessly into the role of King. He really cares about people and when you see him going out amongst crowds and talking to them, you can see he is very much loved. I was watching the VE celebrations the other day and saw him at a tea party at Buckingham Palace, solicitously tucking a blanket round the legs of an elderly lady sitting next to him, which is typical of his thoughtfulness. I also think that Queen Camilla is the most perfect wife for him. He probably thought it would never happen that he would be crowned King, and she would be crowned Queen. I'm so happy for them both and I just can't say how much I love the King and appreciate his friendship.

Kissing

Kissing members of the Royal Family is a very tricky business. You must kiss one cheek, then the other cheek and then curtsy. Well, by the time I've kissed one cheek and then the other I quite often forget about the curtsy, which is a slight problem. Some people do very deep curtsies but if I tried, I'd be terribly worried I'd never get up; clutching onto the poor King and Queen for support, I don't even try and a little bob has to do.

I do think it's very difficult these days to judge whether to kiss people and if so how many times. Some people don't really like to be kissed and sort of back away as one approaches. But in general people kiss much more than when I was a child. Kissing on both cheeks is really a French thing and for some reason it's come over here. When I was with Princess Margaret I think we both resisted it for a while and actually laughed at the double kissing, but then once everyone is doing it, it feels a bit rude not to. The Dutch do it three times which, thank goodness, hasn't caught on here.

Some kisses you look forward to, others are more difficult. What I really hate is at cocktail parties – which I never go to now – when someone who has had slightly too much to drink comes tipping forward and puts their rather sweaty red face firmly on my cheek. I hate that sort of kiss. In fact, at the launch party for my book *Picnic Papers*, one friend had had far too much to drink and came lurching towards me and rather wetly kissed me with an open mouth. Because he is a friend I didn't draw back, but I didn't enjoy it at all. You have to watch out for people like that.

When I'm not well, my darling daughter Amy comes up to help and do odd jobs for me, and then we have a lovely firm kiss on the cheek, that's a kiss I really look forward to.

Kitchen

When I was a child the only time I ever came into the enormous, wonderful kitchen at Holkham was at Christmas. Carey and I were allowed to help stir the Christmas puddings and ice the Christmas cake. Puddings and cakes were given to all the people in the village, the tenant farmers and to the staff. The butler, upper housekeeper and various people like that had one dining room, the kitchen staff and house staff had another and there were cakes and puddings for everyone. I remember we had icing bags and were allowed to ice one cake, which I very much suspect was then redone by Cook, but we were so proud of it.

I suppose I did learn basic cooking at school, how to boil an egg or make a pancake, that sort of thing. But once I was married, we always had a cook. At Glen we had the most marvellous cook called Mrs Walker. I wish I had spent a bit more time with her in the kitchen to watch what she was doing. In those days women had breakfast in bed and Mrs Walker would come up to the bedroom on a Monday morning to go through the list of meals she had planned for the week. Looking back, it was utter luxury. Again, in Mustique we always had a cook, so it really wasn't until Colin went to live in St Lucia and I returned to Norfolk and had no help that I was forced to start to cook for myself. Ironic really as my maiden name was pronounced 'cook'. My mother lived in the same village as me after my father died, and she was very keen on cooking, so she used to come over, or I'd go over to her house and we'd make something together. I still have her recipe book which I treasure. Although my repertoire is rather limited, I think what I produce is perfectly nice.

I'm all for having a substantial breakfast, I love porridge, and then I have two courses for lunch and then I stop eating. Not having dinner has been a revelation to me. I don't get indigestion, I sleep much better and I've taken off the horrible roll of fat round my middle that just seemed to appear overnight in middle age. And my great tip is to cook slightly too much of everything, so you have leftovers. I will cook a whole chicken even if I'm just on my own and make too many vegetables because you can make different dishes with them afterwards. I'm all for leftovers.

Laughter

Laughter is one of the best medicines. Everyone loves to laugh and love the people who make them laugh. My problem is that when I really laugh, I cry, I just can't stop myself. Princess Margaret knew that and, in some situations, often ones where we really shouldn't be laughing, she would just give me a look, and I'd be lost. I'd beg her not to, but she was naughty and sometimes couldn't resist.

I really get the giggles with one of my best friends Tim Leese. We once went on holiday together, driving through France and Italy. His boyfriend had gone back to America, so I seized my chance to have a holiday with him. We went to visit some relatives who lived in a château in France. We had had a rather long drive and were very much looking forward to supper and a drink but when we got to the dining room that evening, there were lots of bottles of wine on the table with little covers like tea cosies on them. It turned out we were supposed to be tasting the wines, giving our opinion and trying to guess where they were all from. Well apart from knowing what I enjoy, I know nothing about wine and was frantically trying to think of things to say as a miserable little half inch of wine was poured into my glass. Tim tried to say that he really couldn't describe the taste as there was so little in his glass, whereupon the host said, 'Yes, I can see you drink rather a lot,' which was frightfully rude, as well as not being true. We both got the most terrible giggles and dared not look at each other. The visit was not a huge success, with rather sparse food on offer, and we decided to leave early one morning to drive on to Italy. However, as we opened the front door two enormous Rottweilers came bounding towards us in an utterly terrifying fashion. We quickly slammed the door shut and realised one of us would have to wake the host. I lost the coin toss and crept up to knock on their bedroom door. Eventually they came down and restrained the dogs and we were able to make our escape. We stopped at the first little bistro we passed and had mountains of toast and eggs and even had a glass of champagne to celebrate our freedom!

Laziness

To me, laziness is the best luxury. I know it might sound ridiculous when I had so many staff, but managing at least two houses with staff and five children, plus looking after Colin and Princess Margaret kept me really busy most of the time. There were always questions to be answered or rows in the household to sort out. But now at my stage in life I'm able to enjoy not doing very much. I still feel a bit guilty when I'm not busy, but I do treasure the ability to be lazy that old age can bring. The other day, it was sunny, and I put my chair out in the garden and made a vodka tonic and sat there with my book and thought to myself, what absolute heaven it was. I have even spotted a particular place in the garden where I can sit and look at my border and I'm going to have a little seat put there so I can enjoy the beautiful flowers. It's an utter treat to have the gift of time and to know the things that make you happy and be able to indulge in them. It's one of the great things about getting old.

Love

I had a certain sympathy with the King when he was the Prince of Wales and asked if he was in love with Diana during their engagement interview, he said, 'whatever in love means'. I think love is complicated. When I was a teenager, curled up in the library at school reading *Wuthering Heights*, I used to fantasise about Heathcliff – I'd dream about being whisked away by him on a white horse. He was my teenage romantic hero so nothing was ever going to live up to him, real life seemed so disappointing in comparison.

I thought I was in love with Johnny Althorp. I was certainly devastated when he married someone else, but I was a child, and we hadn't really spent much time together, so it wasn't real love.

I'm not sure that I can say I was in love with Colin. I thought I was. I was very attracted to him and flattered by his attention, but he was a difficult man. I really wanted to make his life better and help him as I was very fond of him, and he helped me in some ways. I was so young when we were married and almost completely uneducated and he helped educate me, he gave me books he thought I should read and took me to exhibitions, and he was exciting to be around. I think I knew he would be a handful and there was a difficult side to him but in lots of ways he brought adventure into my life. I don't think I would have been very good with the sort of man my father wanted me to marry; probably someone in the Scots Guards with a crumbling castle somewhere. I don't know that Colin was in love with me either, I think he was in love with Clarissa Avon, who was married to Anthony Eden. After Colin's death, Hugo Vickers called me and whilst researching her biography, had come across around two hundred letters from Colin to Clarissa. Among them was a letter he'd written to her from *The Queen Elizabeth* when we were on our honeymoon thanking her for a wedding present in which he says, 'At the church I spent my whole time trying to see where you were sitting.' Nothing about me at all until right at the end when he said, 'Anne did look very beautiful. I felt it was a shame to take her away from Holkham.' I used to blame myself for not loving him enough, but in fact when I read that letter, I realised he didn't really love me. I was a sort of trophy wife; he loved the idea of Holkham and all the things that came with me. I think he was fond of me rather than loved me.

There was another man in my life who taught me what real love felt like, and I'll forever be grateful to him for that. Love should be selfless and about putting the other person first.

I think the purest form of love is the one you feel for your children. From the moment the probably rather hideous, rumpled red-faced baby is put in your arms after you've given birth, the feeling of love is overwhelming. I know there are some people who suffer from post-natal depression and that must be truly terrible, but I was lucky never to feel that and in general, nature is incredible at creating that bond with your child. Today, even when I'm just sent photographs of a new grandchild I look at this tiny, wrinkled person and immediately fall in love with them.

Luck

I've had probably more than my fair share of both good and bad luck. The idea to write a memoir at the age of eighty-seven was a huge stroke of luck. It was just chance that I was at a lunch party and rabbiting away with all my stories and happened to be sitting next to a publisher who suggested I write a book. It was then further good luck that I was put in touch with an excellent agent who found a publisher for it and then the book sold well all over the world. The fact that it was successful was amazing as it came at a point when I had very little money, following on from Colin's extraordinary will in which he left nothing to me or the children. More than just the satisfaction of writing a book people were interested to read, it was also a huge help financially.

I was also very lucky to have been chosen to be Princess Margaret's Lady-in-Waiting and for the Queen to have picked me to be one of her Maids of Honour. Both could have asked other people rather than me, and my life was made so much more interesting by taking on those roles.

But then I've also had the worst luck imaginable with the deaths of two of my sons and darling Christopher's accident. I still worry about something awful happening to the twins and to Christopher again. I think when you have had such bad luck the worry about the potential for other things to go wrong never quite leaves you.

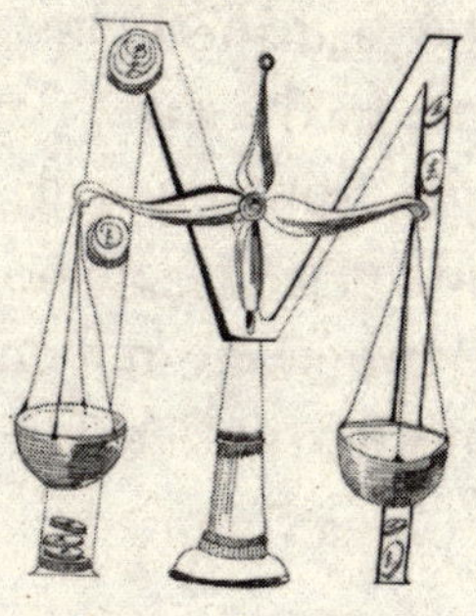

Manners

I think manners is all about thinking about other people, making them feel comfortable, not thinking about oneself. Manners are taught initially in terms of sitting up properly at table, using a knife and fork correctly, and those are the basics. But I think later, good manners are really about things like waiting in a queue, not pushing, exchanging a pleasant word with someone who is serving you in a shop, never being rude. It's all so important for oiling the wheels of society, and people are much more likely to be nice to you if you treat them politely and with good manners. I find it quite shocking when I see visitors here in our local shops being offhand or rude to the people working in them.

My mother was a real stickler for manners. I remember getting into the most terrible trouble one day when someone from the village said they had seen me, and I'd ridden past them on my bike without saying hello. I don't even remember seeing this person, but my mother was furious with me at the time.

Men

I'm aware looking back on the books I've written that men don't always come out of them very well. I think it's true to say I am more of a woman's woman, partly because the women in my life have been the strong ones. I was not particularly close to my father and when I read through his diary, I think it's easy to see why. The most upsetting part of the diary came on the last page when the boat in which my parents were travelling back from Egypt finally docked in Glasgow. They were collected by a car and brought to Downie Park where we were waiting with my nanny and Aunt Bridget to meet them. After three years apart from us, this moment in my father's diary is recorded as 'Jan 20th – arrived Downie. Met by children'. He then goes on to list what he shot two days later: '2 pheasants, 1 pigeon. 1 rabbit. Deep snow'. I still can't quite get over the fact that he didn't even call us by our names, let alone write of any emotion on seeing us. I found that last page quite devastating. There I was at the age of nine longing to see my parents, having been separated from them for three years, and when he met us he shook our hands rather than giving us a hug and he spent more time in his diary listing what he had shot the following day. He never really showed me much love, he was very irritable and rather fussy, obsessed with having the windows open all the time and whether we'd been to the lavatory. There was also the whole business of primogeniture, which didn't endear me to the male of the species! Looking back, I think my father treated me a bit like a son, he was never affectionate with me, although he was more so with my sister who he called his 'little dolly daydreams'. And then, of course, marriage to Colin was not exactly plain sailing. Whereas my mother, my fantastic nanny Barbara Barnes, Princess Margaret and all my wonderful friends were all strong women who I loved spending time with.

Marriage

Despite having had a difficult marriage I still believe in it as an institution. Mainly because I think it's the most stable relationship in which to have children. Partners can just zoom off whereas husbands have to take care of the children, even if its only financially. But I'm under no illusion that marriage is easy, it isn't, and it can be incredibly difficult. I have had one or two friends who had the most wonderful marriages, but I would say they are probably the exception rather than the rule. Happily, Christopher and May are both in very happy marriages and I'm so grateful for that.

Money

It was common practice when I got married that a girl's father would give her a 'dowry', some money of her own to use as pocket money during the marriage. For some reason, under the influence of a dreadful lawyer who worked for my father, he decided not to give either Carey or me any money, which was appallingly mean of him. My mother gave me a little bit, but my father-in-law kindly gave me a small sum instead, which I found very embarrassing. Money became a source of difficulty in our marriage. Colin was incredibly extravagant and burnt through his inheritance so that by the time he died he was more or less bankrupt. He spent far more than he could afford on Mustique, not only in the building of it, but also in throwing glamorous parties where he hired aeroplanes to fly people out and imported clothes from India. I knew we couldn't really afford it and consequently never really enjoyed the parties. The final straw of course was when he left what little money was left to Kent, his manservant.

As a result, I've always been very careful with

money. When I was younger, I worked in a shop selling Holkham Pottery and enjoyed that but when I was with Colin I didn't work. Suddenly, finding myself in a position where I was making my own money through writing at the age of eighty-seven has made me very happy and proud. Of course, then I learnt about the horrors of tax but at least I had earned enough money to be paying tax. I do think it's so important where at all possible for women to earn their own money in a relationship, most do these days but in my time it was rare. Both of my daughters are very careful with what they earn.

Mustique and Kate Moss

One of the real joys of Mustique has been the friendship we formed with the singer Bryan Adams. He became a great friend and was very kind to Colin, even composing and performing a song for his funeral. Bryan is a very strict vegan and doesn't go out much on Mustique, but the last time I was there he called to say that Kate Moss was keen to meet me and would I like to go over for brunch. She was staying on the island with some girlfriends to celebrate her birthday so of course I went along. She was charming, and we got along very well, chatting away together. Bryan gave us these very healthy green smoothies which were nice but when he had to pop out Kate looked at me and said, 'Shall we go and get a drink?' I quickly said yes even though it was only eleven o'clock in the morning. Off we went to Basil's bar, and she was so nice and the most tremendous fun. We had a lovely time and I suddenly realised we'd drunk three Mustique Mules, and it was hardly lunchtime!

When Bryan came to play at a concert in Thetford

Forest here in Norfolk, he very kindly invited the children and me along. We found him in his trailer before the performance where someone was doing his hair and getting him ready. He'd said that we could watch from the back of the stage, so the twins and I followed him on his walk from the trailer and my goodness what a change as he walked onto the stage. He's actually a very charming, rather mild-mannered man but as he went out to perform, he morphed into the rock star that he is, full of energy and playing the most amazing guitar solos. It was a terrific evening and we all had a great time, I'm very fond of him.

Nannies

Whoever looks after children will have an impact on them and I had both horrid and lovely nannies when I was growing up. Billy Williams was the nanny who looked after us following a really dreadful nanny we had whilst my parents were abroad. Billy was wonderful and came with us when we went to live near Chester in Cheshire for a time when my father was sent there by his regiment. She knew I loved the book *The Secret Garden* and created a space in our garden which only she and I knew about. It was the most thoughtful gesture and I think being in that little private space really helped me to heal after the abuse I'd suffered from the previous nanny.

There was a whole etiquette to the nanny scene,

and we all treated our nannies very well, we knew how important they were. When Barbara Barnes used to have other nannies and their children staying at Glen for meals, she would seat them in order of importance at the table in the nursery in the same way that we did in the dining room downstairs. The most senior nanny would be seated to Barbara's right; often that would be Princess Margaret's nanny who was called Nanny Sumner. They would have a glass of sherry or later, wine. I put my foot down at champagne as I said even we weren't having champagne, but they all had a very nice time. The poor kitchen maid would stagger up to the nursery with trays groaning with food for the visiting nannies and woe betide if she was late. I used to dread Barbara asking me for a word to say she was sorry to report that the nursery supper had been brought up ten minutes late again.

When Princess Diana got rid of Barbara she went to work for a very smart children's clothes shop, Young England, on Elizabeth Street, which I always thought was such a clever idea. I am quite sure there were customers who were thrilled to be advised and served by the former nanny to Princes William and Harry. This would have been even more the case when she took the clothes to New York and, whilst staying in a smart hotel, would sell to rich Americans who were enthralled to hear what the Royal children were wearing.

Naughtiness

It's great fun to be a bit naughty occasionally but any unkind naughtiness needs to be stopped. I was always rather a good child, I think because I was punished so severely by this awful nanny for any minor transgression that I didn't ever want to do anything very naughty. When we were younger at Holkham we all had to wait for everyone to arrive at breakfast before we were allowed to start eating, and the worst thing we did was steal the odd grape or two from the table. Similarly, raiding the raspberries in the kitchen garden at our boarding school was another bit of fruit related pilfering! I suppose I might be guilty of what could be called social naughtiness, occasionally scurrying off in the opposite direction if you see someone you don't want to talk to at a party, but I think that's probably about as bad as I get.

Neighbours

When I was growing up we didn't really have neighbours. People who lived in stately homes often didn't as the houses were surrounded by land and weren't close to anyone other than those who lived and worked on the Estate. Of course we did have neighbours in London. At Hill House we threw a coming out party for Amy and May in the garden. It was a wonderful evening with a band and an amazing structure Colin had imported from India. We invited all the neighbours but the people opposite never replied to our invitation and halfway through the party came storming over, banging on the door, demanding we turn the music off. Of course, Colin completely ignored them and a little later the police came knocking and we had to bring everyone inside.

I really value my neighbours in the countryside; they are so kind and attentive. A Swedish family moved into the village and even came over with a cake they had baked. I was a bit taken aback so popped round to theirs with a signed copy of my book; it was all I could think of to return the favour!

Newspapers

I love physical copies of newspapers, I'm rather old-fashioned like that, and I don't enjoy looking at them on an iPad. I do the crosswords each morning, the easy ones I might add, and it's a lovely start to the day. I read the *Telegraph* to see who's died, and what the Royal Family are doing; the Court Circular interests me very much as I can imagine what is involved in their various appointments. And I really enjoy the *Daily Mail*, it's very gossipy but it's good fun and they have been a friend to me in my career as an author. I have had terrible times with newspapers in the past, particularly when Charlie and Henry were ill and Christopher had his accident, but in recent years they have generally been kind and supportive of me for which I'm grateful.

Noise

I live quite close to the RAF air base at Lakenheath and occasionally there is a tremendous roar as a jet flies low overhead. I don't mind it at all; I actually find it rather comforting to think they are there protecting us. Quite often when I hear them, I find out afterwards that a Russian plane has flown into our airspace and the planes have been scrambled to see it off.

A few years ago there was a small airstrip behind my house that was sometimes used by people coming in for shooting parties at Holkham, but then all sorts of small aircraft started coming in at night. They would cut their engines over the village to glide into land, but because my house is slightly raised up, they would suddenly have to kick the engines into life again to lift up over it. It was infuriatingly noisy and I got very fed up with being woken up. I called the police who refused to do anything about it until one day a couple of policemen happened to be in the lane and saw the planes coming into land. I told them that I was planning to go up there and confront the pilots about it. However, the police made me promise not to act and instead set up cameras in the woods to try and film what was going on. They discovered that the planes were bringing in drugs from Holland so the authorities put a stop to it and I wasn't woken up by planes at night again.

Opera

I've always been very keen on opera, I think partly because my grandfather loved it and used to play me opera choruses in the long gallery at Holkham. Before I met Colin, I went out with an opera singer called Nigel Leigh Pemberton who sang under the name Nigel Douglas for the Welsh National Opera. When we were courting we used to go to Covent Garden to see the opera; like the cinema, it offered a chance to sit really close and hold hands. It was as intimate as we were allowed to get. I particularly liked Wagner's Ring Cycle because it was so long, our hands were almost numb by the time we emerged. Our relationship ended when he went off to sing in Germany, but we stayed friends. After Colin and I were married, Nigel was staying with us at Glen when he was called by someone at the Edinburgh Festival who needed a replacement to take over the title role in Peter Grimes at about three hours' notice. It was very exciting and rather high stakes as he had never performed the role in English up to that point, only in German. We all went up with him to watch and it's probably lucky he didn't know that the composer, Benjamin Britten, was sitting in the audience. He was then invited by Britten to sing in one of his operas at the Aldeburgh Festival.

My father used to take me to the Aldeburgh Festival at Snape Maltings, it was one of the few activities we could enjoy together and which brought us closer. He never took my mother or sister, who were less interested in opera, so it was particularly special for me. I still love going to the opera when I can, *Madam Butterfly* is a particular favourite of mine, and I have always enjoyed going to Glyndebourne where I was great friends with George Christie whose father founded the opera festival, and his wife Mary.

I have managed to convert my daughter May to opera. Previously neither of the twins had been very keen but May came with me when I was invited to visit Vienna to see *Der Rosenkavalier*. It's the perfect opera to see in Vienna, where it is set, and it was the most magical experience. We stayed in the Sacher Hotel, which is one of the most beautiful hotels I think I have ever stayed in. I certainly didn't notice noise from any neighbouring rooms, and I could practically touch the opera house from my bedroom window. When we arrived for the opera I noticed everyone was very nicely dressed, not in black tie or anything that formal but all the men were wearing suits and the women in pretty dresses. We were taken to a little table where we found two glasses of champagne and some delicious nibbles, which we enjoyed before being taken to our front-row seats. I was a bit worried as sometimes the front row is just too close, but in fact this wasn't because we could see the whole orchestra and the conductor, and it was completely fascinating, plus we had an excellent view of the entire stage. In the second interval we returned to a different numbered table where we found two glasses of rosé and some tiny Sachertorte cakes sitting on a tray. When the third interval came along there were two glasses of water waiting for us. I think they thought we'd had quite enough alcohol by that point. The opera with all those wonderful waltzes was just beautiful and May adored it. Now she is planning to accompany me to the other opera visits I have planned, to Glyndebourne and to see *Don Pasquale* which is being performed at Holkham where they stage an opera every year.

Outdoors

I'm very lucky to have a little wooden hut in my garden with double doors, a small table where I can put a cup of tea or vodka tonic and a chair with a cushion. I sit in there with the sun flooding in on a summer's day and it's just perfect. When the weather is fine I usually go into the garden before breakfast, generally barefoot and look at all my plants, noting which ones will need a bit of special attention and watering that evening.

I go for a walk every day, either to the beach or around the lake at Holkham. I'm really spoilt for lovely places to go. I know there's a lot talked about mental health at the moment, and for me being outside and going for a walk is the greatest balm for the soul. However, what I can't bear is talk of being in 'nature'. I don't really understand what it means, for me it's just about being outside, whether it's a park in a town or in the countryside, somewhere where you can walk on grass or sit under a tree.

One of the things Princess Margaret liked to do when she came to stay with me in Norfolk in the spring was to go to Sandringham where the rhodo-dendrons and azaleas were out. Her great treat was to take a picnic over there and if the weather was fine, to sit by this huge golden Buddha. The statue had been given to the Prince of Wales, later Edward VII, as a housewarming gift by Admiral Sir Henry Keppel who had been stationed in China. Princess Margaret loved its patina, and we all had to stroke it the whole time, which was a little odd. I've heard recently that now the garden is open to the public apparently that's what everyone likes to do, I can only imagine the poor old Buddha is getting rather worn.

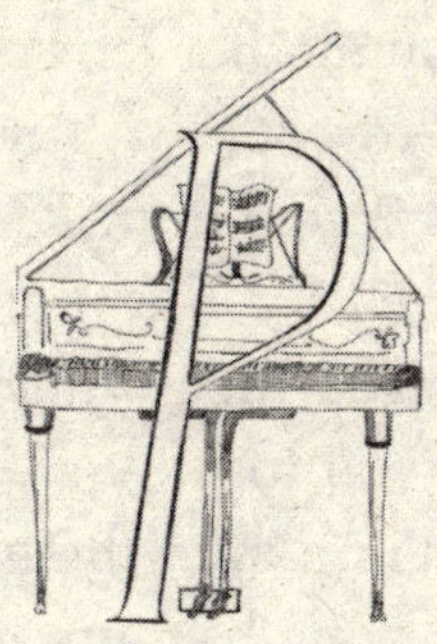

Packing

I've become rather adept at packing – both grand
packing from days with Princess Margaret as well as
the more mundane kind from all of our trips to
Mustique. But the first thing I really remember is
packing for boarding school. We all had these huge
trunks with our names on and at the beginning I
was fascinated by everything because we had so many
uniforms and outfits for different occasions. My
mother's lady's maid helped me pack it with tissue
paper and it was all rather exciting until I was taken
to Holkham station and put on the train for boarding
school and suddenly felt the horror and sadness of
being sent away.

I remember when I first went to stay at Windsor

Castle for Ascot my mother lent me her lady's maid to come with me to cope with the five changes of clothes we were expected to make in a day. Different outfits were required for the morning, then lunch, then Ascot, drinks and then dinner. The lady's maid would travel with you to look after your clothes, to wash and pack and iron everything. They might even help with putting your hair up and would lay out all the clothes for you ready for each change.

When I became a lady-in-waiting I had to buy a whole array of new luggage: cases and hat boxes and something separate for shoes. If we went away on an official trip, it was all marvellous as your luggage would be whisked away and you only saw it again once everything had been unpacked for you at your destination. But when Princess Margaret came to stay in Mustique, or with me in Norfolk, she didn't bring her maid, so it was my job to pack for her. Her packing was in very grand, huge leather trunks which had shelves inside that lifted out like trays, to keep things separate. Everything was wrapped in acid-free tissue paper and it was all very elaborate. I think she used to quite enjoy sitting on the bed watching me on my knees packing everything up for her whilst she instructed what item was to go where. In the diary I have recently discovered, my father writes of embarking on their journey back from Egypt in 1941 with forty-three pieces of luggage weighing a total of two and a half tons —

travel with Princess Margaret was never quite that bad.

Packing to go away is much simpler now although I'm still not very good at packing light, I tend to take too much. When I go to Mustique we change in the evening into long kaftans, but I've got quite good at squeezing everything in. Someone gave me the tip of rolling my clothes which has been very helpful, and I stick to cotton clothes and steer clear of linen which creases dreadfully.

Photography

Photography has been one of my passions ever since my grandfather gave me a Box Brownie camera and taught me how to develop my own prints. He had a darkroom at Holkham and I can recall the excitement of watching as the photographs gradually revealed themselves. I've been fairly systematic about putting the prints into albums and now have over one hundred photograph albums, which has been very helpful when I've been writing my books. I didn't keep diaries, so the photographs have helped to trigger memories of events and people. I worry in this digital world that people forget to print out their photographs and although they take masses of snaps, it's really the prints that stay with you.

I'm very fortunate to have been photographed by many of the best-known photographers from the 1960s to the 1980s, most of whom I got to know quite well. I loved Cecil Beaton who took a photograph of us Maids of Honour before the Coronation in white dresses. We had to go to Fishmongers' Hall to have it taken and I remember it as a very special day.

He was such a fascinating character, quite difficult but so interesting and funny and I think took the most magical photographs. My father engaged up-and-coming photographer, Tony Snowdon, whom he called Tony Snapshot, to take the photographs at my wedding. This was before Tony knew Princess Margaret and at a time when photographers were socially on a par with butchers, bakers and candlestick makers. Poor Tony wasn't invited to the wedding lunch, and I think had his alone on a tray somewhere. I'm afraid he always minded about that. But he had great charm, and he took a wonderful photograph at my wedding where I am standing at the top of the marble staircase at Holkham with my dress fanned out around me and the light is beautiful. I tried to have the shot recreated when May was married at Holkham and was photographed by Patrick Lichfield, who is also a cousin of mine and another excellent photographer, but I felt his photographs didn't have quite the same magic. David Bailey I think was more used to taking photographs of models and actresses and I found it quite difficult to relax in front of him. I was so uptight I think he thought I was covered in barbed wire! But we all loved Robert Mapplethorpe who took some interesting photographs of the twins and a rather amazing photograph of Charlie, who I think he might have been quite in love with, all dressed in black leather lying on a sofa.

Piano

I would have loved to have been able to play the piano properly, it's one of the regrets I have that I didn't persevere with it. My sister Carey and I were taught at Holkham by a teacher who came from Wells. She had a ruler that she would rap our knuckles with when we made a mistake. I hated it and got about as far as being able to play 'The Merry Peasant' and then stopped. Princess Margaret played the piano beautifully. She loved Ethel Merman songs or Danny Kaye; she really loved Danny Kaye. When we were in Scotland at Glen she might play Scottish country tunes, and we'd all sing round the piano. Colin also used to play, he wasn't as good as her, but he wasn't bad, and I enjoyed it when he was at the piano. I've always thought there is something very sexy about a man playing the piano, if he's playing well, it really doesn't matter what he looks like it's just very attractive. When he was playing the piano it made me look at Colin in a more affectionate light, the moment he left the piano I'm afraid those feelings evaporated.

Poetry

The time I really enjoyed poetry was at boarding school during the war when we had this wonderful English teacher called Miss Ball. She used to take us out into the orchard in the summer, and we would lie under the apple and pear trees, and she'd stroke our legs while reading us poems by Siegfried Sassoon. I'm sure it would be totally unacceptable now but back then it all seemed completely heavenly. Other than that, I enjoy the sort of poetry which you can recite and has rhythm and rhyme but I'm not very good with some modern poetry which I find hard to understand.

Colin's oldest uncle, who was called Edward Tennant but whom everyone knew as 'Bim', was killed in the trenches at just nineteen. He wrote poetry from a very young age, including some during the war. After his death, his mother Pamela Glenconner collected the poems and published a memoir about him. I think one that he wrote about her when he was only five is really charming.

I know a face, a lovely face, as full of beauty as of
  grace,
A face of pleasure, ever bright, in utter darkness it
  gives light,
A face that is itself like joy, to have seen it I'm a
  lucky boy.
But I've a joy that have few other, this lovely woman
  is my mother.

Pottery

My mother's passion for pottery is well known, having started Holkham Pottery which is sadly now closed. But she also ignited a similar passion in Prince Charles when he came to stay with us. She showed him how to throw a pot at Holkham and subsequently sent him books on pottery when he was away at school. I have many wonderful letters he wrote to my mother from Gordonstoun thanking her for books or pieces of pottery she had sent, and telling her about the pots he was working on with the help of a new young master, who was clearly sympathetic. He obviously enjoyed it immensely and writes of trying to create a set of soup bowls but worrying that they would crack as soon as the soup was poured in, and of the excitement of improving his throwing on one of the three pottery wheels in the art department.

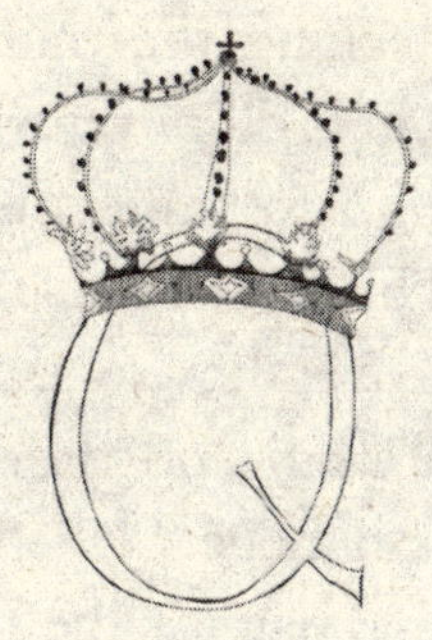

Queen

I remember when I heard the news of the Queen's death I just burst into tears. We knew she hadn't been well and that it would happen at some point but there was this incredible sadness, which I think the whole country felt. The queues of people who waited to pass by her coffin are testament to how much she was loved and respected, and how much she was a part of everyone's lives. She had been part of mine for such a long time. I'd known her since she was eight or nine and when she chose me to be her Maid of Honour at the Coronation, she was responsible for giving me the most incredible day of my life. We all felt very proud of the role we played in trying to help her feel as comfortable as she could be on that day, checking the train didn't drag and arranging it round her. I'll never forget the moment she was anointed, and we were among the very few people to see it. The cameras had been turned off and a canopy put over her so that it was only us, the Duke of Edinburgh and the bishops who saw, and it was such a privilege. She stuck to the promises she made on that day for the rest of her life; she really was just extraordinary. Occasionally I look at my Coronation dress and at the brooch she gave me, and the memories of that whole amazing day come flooding back.

I think in the end Queen Elizabeth got on very well with the current Queen. They both love dogs and horses and really had quite a lot in common. I've always been a fan of Queen Camilla, I think she and the King are so well-suited and she does a marvellous job in supporting him. Colin and I were invited to their wedding which had to be delayed by twenty-four hours in order that Charles could attend the funeral of Pope John Paul II on behalf of the Queen. That meant that the wedding took place on the day of the Grand National, which wasn't ideal for the Queen who was such a keen follower of horse racing. At the party afterwards Colin and I made sure we were standing near the cake and were in prime position to see the Queen giving the most wonderful speech in which she compared the course of their relationship to the racecourse at Aintree, with the couple having cleared all the obstacles in their path, crossing the finishing line and now finally enjoying being in the winners' enclosure. As soon as she'd finished the speech and the cake was cut however, we noticed she beetled off to watch the race.

The current Queen was also the person who encouraged me to write about the domestic abuse I'd suffered in my second book *Whatever Next*. She is very involved with domestic abuse charities and knew I'd had a difficult marriage. She felt that it would help others to talk about their experiences if I shared mine. I think sometimes people don't realise that abuse can happen at every level of society. I'm grateful to her for prompting me to do it as the letters I received subsequently made me realise that it has helped other people to hear about my experiences.

Queer Uncles

Darling Uncle Roger used to live with us at Holkham. There were often gay uncles and unmarried aunts living in stately homes because back then homosexuality was illegal and relatives would feel safer living with their family in a large house rather than on their own. Uncle Roger had his own house, but he used to come and eat with us every evening and stay overnight, eventually he was given his own flat in a wing at Holkham. He clearly had a boyfriend as he was eventually left a huge estate in Norfolk, but it was so much easier for him to live with us and meant he didn't have to employ any staff. We loved having him around and there was plenty of space. There were also spinster aunts sitting around in corners who would be knitting. Another great aunt, Marjorie, also used to stay with us and because meals were sometimes rather long and rather boring, she carried around a radio which she'd turn on and put under her chair. It made my great grandmother very cross: 'Marjorie will you please turn your wireless off, we are supposed to be having stimulating conversation!'

When my son Henry told us he was gay, I think I perhaps found it harder than Colin. I felt that it had been irresponsible of him to have got married and have a son, Euan, whom he was now going to leave. I thought it was very sad for him, but his wife Tessa was so good about it, and they stayed close friends right up until Henry died. I begged him to be careful as when he came out the AIDS epidemic was reaching its height, but of course he wasn't and ended up contracting and dying of the disease. I've already written about that time and won't go into it again, but it is a truly terrible disease and I'm so pleased that it is no longer a death sentence.

Queues

I dreaded queues when I was married to Colin as he took absolutely no notice of them and used to stride up to the front, ignoring everyone. What was remarkable was how little he was ever challenged on it. I quite wished someone would shout at him, but it never happened. I was often trailing in his wake, dreadfully embarrassed but not wanting to provoke an argument. Of course queues are important and prevent people being trampled underfoot. I'm very happy to wait my turn, although the old impatience creeps in when I'm queuing in traffic.

Reading

Reading has completely saved me at different points in my life. When I was young, I was sent away to boarding school and was terribly homesick. I just didn't understand why after having been away from me for three years in the war, my parents were then sending me away again. I thought I must be irritating them. But the school library was my refuge; it had this big window seat with a curtain you could pull round you and I used to curl up with a book for hours. I went through all the classics and in particular loved Jane Austen, *Wuthering Heights* and the *Cranford* series by Elizabeth Gaskell. They were pure escapism and such a comfort to me, really helping me to get through the misery of being separated from my parents. I suppose in those days we didn't have television or the internet to distract us, so books and friendship were vital.

Colin was a voracious reader and introduced me to all sorts of interesting books, mainly non-fiction. But I also used books as an escape from him occasionally, when I'd run off to a little caravan I'd bought and installed in the woods at Glen. He didn't know it was there and when I was feeling stressed or overwhelmed, I'd slink off to it, pull the red gingham curtains, sink into the knitted cushions and lose myself in a novel. Only Nanny Barbara knew where I was, and would fetch me if it was urgent, but otherwise I was in complete heaven. I still read a lot today, quite apart from reading the newspaper every day, and am sent books to read and give quotes on which can be fun. I think reading has been the thing, other than my children, which has given me the most pleasure in my life.

Religion

Religion has always been a part of my life. When I was younger and living at Holkham we went to prayers in the chapel every morning, and every night we knelt by our beds to say the Lord's Prayer. It was very much part of the fabric of our lives. Lots of the books we had as children were religious. I remember one of my first picture books had a picture of Jesus with a huge halo and animals round him. But faith really came into focus in my life when Christopher had his accident and Charlie and Henry died. I had a spiritual experience at the hands of a Christian healer called Mrs Black who helped me and Christopher enormously at that time.

Religion, like politics, is one of those things you aren't supposed to talk about at dinner parties, but the older I get the more I think 'why not?' Especially now when religious wars are tearing the world apart. It's so sad that something which should be wonderful and healing can cause so much suffering and I think we should talk about it.

I love going to my church here in Burnham Thorpe

and when I can't get there on a Sunday I feel rather guilty. But if I can't make it, sometimes I say a little prayer in my garden, and I think that is just as good. Our lovely church can smell a bit musty so sometimes praying outside is preferable. The last time I was there was for a funeral and it was not long after I'd had my cataracts done so my eyesight was better than it had been. I was kneeling to pray and to my horror spotted some mould at the base of a pillar, it was practically sprouting weeds! As soon as the funeral was over out came the scrubbing brush and the bleach.

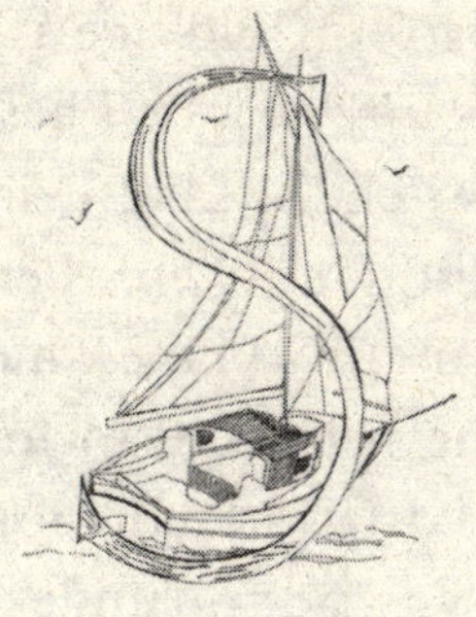

Sailing and Swimming

Two of my favourite forms of exercise and relaxation. Following a capsize at sea when I was eighty, I have retired from sailing, but for seventy-five years it brought me enormous pleasure. My mother was also a keen sailor. She used to go off with the Duke of Edinburgh who had a boat he used to sail from the Royal Yacht *Britannia* when they were on tour. Sailing is rather like hunting in that people's language in boats can be appalling. There are also lots of rules to master, like who gives way to whom in certain wind conditions, the names of the various ropes and the best knots to tie in different situations, it can be all encompassing, and I love it.

Swimming is something you can really do at any

age, and particularly in old age it's rather good as you aren't bearing any weight. These days the North Sea feels a bit too chilly. Like Princess Margaret, I was spoilt by Mustique where there were beautiful beaches and I swam the whole time. It was paradise, the corals and the fish were so lovely, and I spent hours with an old-fashioned snorkel taking it all in. I only wish I'd had an underwater camera. It was a magical time. There was also the added benefit that Colin did not like swimming, following the tragic drowning of a friend of his at Oxford, so it was a moment when I had time to myself.

I also swam with Princess Margaret in the pool at Buckingham Palace which had been redone after the war. It felt hugely luxurious, with fluffy towels lined up and talcum powder in the changing room. I would swim on my side chatting to her as she performed a stately breaststroke up and down the pool, both of us trying not to get our hair wet.

One of the gifts of getting older is being able to give up the things that you never really enjoyed but perhaps did for the sake of the children. Skiing would come into that category for me; I never loved it and at some point lost my nerve, as I increasingly worried about being crashed into by other skiers and hurting myself. Similarly, riding, which I did as a child and loved my own pony, but was always slightly terrified by any new horse I had to ride. I realise it's a real privilege to have had the opportunity to try all these things but in the end swimming and sailing have been my real passions.

Sex

I knew I couldn't write a book like this without including sex. People talk about sex all the time these days, but I'm of an age and generation who wouldn't dream of talking to anyone about it. My friends and I might well say we thought someone was sexy, but we'd never ever talk about the act of sex itself. None of us slept with our boyfriends, we were very naive and things only really changed with the advent of oral contraception. I certainly knew nothing about sex and what to expect. All my mother had told me was to watch what the dogs did. We had a vague idea, but because we had so little concrete information, we made things up in our head and had the most horrific stories we'd tell each other. The wedding night came as something of a shock for all of us. I've written about my terrible honeymoon with the trip to a Paris brothel that was perfectly disgusting. I rather wish I had been more aware and think that if I had been, perhaps my marriage to Colin would have got off to an easier start.

Because we never slept with people before we

were married, we had no idea whether we were sexually compatible with them. There were a few happy marriages but lots of people were unfaithful, almost as though they were doing their experimenting and trying to find a compatible partner from the safety net of a marriage. Divorce wasn't really an option, it was very much frowned upon and you were expected to produce heirs and spares to inherit a title. So, if things weren't brilliant in bed with your husband or wife the temptation was to look elsewhere. Colin had lots of affairs, and in the end I found someone who made me very happy, but I never seriously considered leaving the marriage, even in the most difficult of times. I do think that in general it's much better that there is more openness about sex now and that people sleep together before they get married so they can make a more informed decision about who they want to spend their life with.

Secrets

Some people are very bad at keeping secrets. I know that I sometimes let things slip that I shouldn't, but I don't think I've ever revealed an important secret. There are one or two friends who know things about me that they would never tell. Equally I know things about friends that will stay with me to the grave. I think sharing a secret builds trust and can be the glue that cements a friendship. I suspect I would never have been chosen to be a lady-in-waiting if I hadn't been thought to be a trustworthy person. I think that's probably why the Queen liked my book. There were lots of funny little stories in it that people might not have known but nothing that would cause any serious embarrassment to the family. There are certainly things I know that I would never tell.

Shopping

I never really liked shopping, not in England in any case. The only sort of shopping I absolutely loved was in India with my friend Margaret Vyner. That was wonderful. Partly because taxis were incredibly cheap so we could hire a taxi for the day which would wait outside shops for us and take us on to the next place. Plus, there were so many exciting and beautiful things to look at and choose from, it was heavenly. What I hate is all the traipsing about, walking for hours or failing to find a taxi when you are exhausted. Shopping in India was never like that. Now I absolutely hate clothes shopping and rely on mail-order brochures or the occasional trip into Norwich with my daughter-in-law, Johanna, where there is one store that contains several concessions so I can stay in one place. I loathe trying things on in changing rooms which are usually too small and with nowhere to sit. It's no fun anymore.

The only sort of shopping I do enjoy is at little local shops for food and other bits and pieces. I've got a wonderful fish shop and a butcher and greengrocers, they are all great and I like going into them and having a quick chat with whoever is serving. And there's one shop I adore called 'This and That' in Wells-next-the-Sea. They sell anything you could possibly want from photograph frames to nails and screws and perfectly good cheap crackers at Christmas. Apart from food and clothes, I can get everything I need from there.

Sitting Straight

My grandmother was very strict but I'm grateful she was such a stickler for good posture as it's really helped me in my old age. She used to make us sit at lunch with broom handles down our backs, which wasn't much fun at the time but has served me well. I've been told by a doctor that my spine is very straight and that I don't have any of the calcium deposits that can build up in your spine at my age. I know it's tricky to avoid but I do worry that the younger generation hunching over their phones and computers are storing up problems for their later life.

Sport

I was very competitive at school sports. Netball was my favourite, I played goal attack and relished barging my way through to the goal. I was quite tall and strong and a useful player. My mother had also been very good at sports, and I remember feeling very proud when she used to come to school sports day and compete in the mothers' tennis matches. But I really hated cricket which we were also made to play. The only decent roles as far as I could see were batting and bowling, and I was never good enough to get a proper crack at those so was always put to field somewhere miles away. I'd see this very hard red ball flying towards me and hear the cries of 'Catch it, Coke' and then had to endure the agony when I invariably dropped the catch.

The only sport I carried on with after school was tennis, which I loved. There used to be this rather wonderful tennis club behind Marble Arch near Tyburn Convent where I would play with a group of friends, some of whom were much better than me which helped to up my game. My daughters are also very good at tennis which is such a lovely social game. I carried on playing until well into my seventies when I decided I just couldn't run fast enough.

Stairs

My trick for keeping healthy is to use the stairs even when there is another option. I never use a lift or an escalator if I can help it, instead I'll go and find the back stairs. It can be a rather useful habit in a department store as there's often a loo on the way if I need a break. In the mornings I carry my breakfast tray up to my bedroom making sure I walk up the stairs without holding onto the handrail, as previously discussed I try never to use handrails.

When Carey and I were sent to Scotland our bedrooms and the nursery were at the top of the house and my cousin Jamie and Carey, who were quite naughty, were often caught swooshing down the bannisters. They couldn't help themselves, shrieking with the excitement of it, which of course brought out my governess and Jamie's nanny to see what was going on, and they got a frightful telling off. It was very dangerous but the most tremendous fun.

Telephones

I do have a mobile which I take with me in my car in case I break down but in general I don't use it and rely on my landline. I have a complicated relationship with the telephone. I am often at home on my own and love speaking to friends or my daughters when they call, but I get very troubled if I receive a call either late at night or early in the morning. I remember when Christopher had his accident in Belize his friend called me in the middle of the night to tell me; it was a dreadful moment. I also have one or two fans in Australia and sometimes they call at very odd times. One particular fan has not got the idea of the time difference at all and calls me in the middle of the night. 'Hello, Lady Glenconner, I'm just calling to see how you are?' I said, 'I'm not best pleased because you've called me in the middle of the night.' I'm afraid he got the sharp end of my tongue, and he hasn't done it since.

My generation is less good with phones. We only had one telephone at Holkham which was in a draughty passage so you never wanted to chat for long as it was freezing cold, and you certainly couldn't say anything private. In those days people wrote letters more and the telephone was just for making arrangements. Today, people spend their whole time glued to their mobile phones. I've finally upgraded my landline handset from my very old Bakelite one to something more modern.

Therapy

Everyone seems to have therapy these days, some people even take their therapist on holiday with them. That seems a little excessive, but there have been a couple of times in my life when I have used therapy and found it to be incredibly helpful.

When darling Henry died of AIDS we had an awful time with the press. They rang on the doorbell at all hours in London, they hounded Henry's son at his school and chased after us down the street, it was a total nightmare, and at a time when we were desperately grieving for him. I was so tired and kept bursting into tears, so my local vicar suggested that it might help for me to have someone outside the family to talk to. It seemed like a sensible idea, and he kindly found me a woman who lived quite close by. I went to talk to her, only for a couple of weeks but I found it hugely helpful to have that outside perspective and to be able to say things I couldn't or wouldn't want to say to my family or friends.

Colin had a therapist who sadly died and so for a while I became a surrogate therapist for him. He used to lie on the floor in a foetal position keeping me awake all night, it was dreadful. I asked my doctor what I could do, and he suggested I go and see a therapist myself to learn about therapy, a bit like being at therapy school, so I could help Colin. He sent me to see a wonderful woman called Dr Nina Colthard. It was really to talk about Colin, but she ended up asking about me and I told her all about the dreadful governess I'd had as a child. What was extraordinary was that I became physically paralysed when I was talking about it, I was lying down but I couldn't move. The horror of it was manifesting itself in this very physical way. I did feel better after talking everything through with her and although I was only with her for a short time, it was enough for me to be able to carry on and to be useful to Colin.

I never wanted to continue with therapy long term, but those two short stints were very helpful, and I can see why talking to a professional can offer real benefits.

Tidying

I know it's a cliché but I truly believe that a tidy house means a tidy mind. I love tidying and really can't bear it when things are in a mess. Being tidy allows me to think more clearly. In a way I think I had tidied away all the stories from my past in my mind and when I was writing my books I found I had excellent recall and could just unlock the memories, which came flooding back.

When my grandchildren come to stay, I never even look into their rooms, I just can't, you can hardly get in the door for all the clothes and dirty knickers all over the floor. I really mind about dirty knickers on the floor; they should be put in a laundry basket. When I was growing up my grandmother taught us that if you hang up your clothes just after you have taken them off the warmth from your body means that all the creases fall out, whereas if you leave them in a pile on the floor they just end up looking crumpled and messy. I suppose with modern fabrics that might be less the case, but I think it's a good rule of thumb to live by.

Twins

I always longed for girls, having had three boys, but when I found out I was having twins I burst into tears. I was convinced I'd be having boys and was exhausted at the thought of it all. The other issue was that at the time I discovered it was considered terribly common to have multiple births. It's ridiculous I know, but everyone kept telling me, especially my sister, which didn't make me feel better about the whole situation. Today with IVF there are more multiple births but it was fairly unusual back then, particularly among my friends. Luckily my lovely nanny Barbara was excited at the prospect and took charge, finding a wonderful twin pram for sale in *The Lady* magazine. It cost a fortune and was absolutely huge, with room for Christopher and the twins. I could hardly move it, but Barbara proudly wheeled it round the gardens and into the park.

When the twins arrived and they were girls I was really thrilled, no matter how common it was considered! I'm relieved I didn't have triplets though. Colin had come up with their pretty names – Amy and

May – and I'm not sure Yam or Yma, or any other anagram of their names would have quite cut the mustard. I had a wonderful maternity nurse who came for the first six months to help. She was a Roman Catholic and insisted on having Sunday off to go to church, which made Barbara quite sniffy. Only one of my good friends had twins but I always feel I have a tremendous connection with other women who've had multiple births. I don't know how people cope with twin babies when they don't have lots of help like I did, I'm full of sympathy and admiration for mothers in that situation.

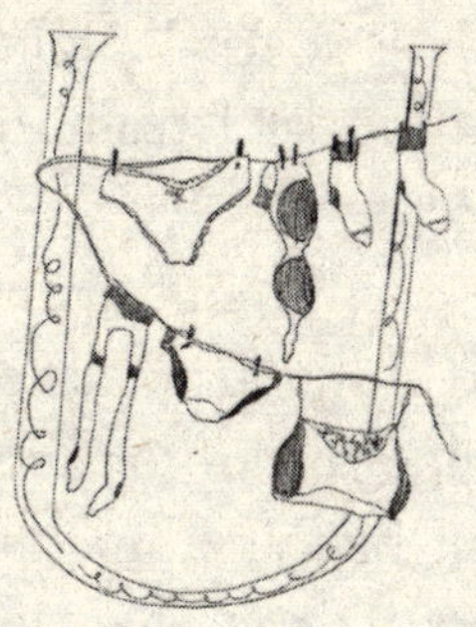

Underwear

I remember Colin once giving me what he thought was sexy underwear. I didn't enjoy wearing it and didn't find it at all comfortable. What I really love is big pants. I adore the scene in the first Bridget Jones film where she comes flying down the fireman's pole with her big pants on display. That's my kind of underwear, lovely and comfortable. I always get mine from Marks and Spencer's, along with my bras. I've never been a Rigby and Peller, luxurious lingerie kind of person. I always get the same M & S bra in white, with one or two black ones for wearing with darker evening dresses. The only other item I have is a boned bodysuit to try and pull in my tummy but it's such a bind to wear. It's got all these poppers

181

underneath which is a total nightmare when you need to go to the loo, so I really try not to wear it very often.

The only time I enjoyed expensive lingerie was when I went into hospital to have the children. In those days they kept you in for about ten days, after which you'd be in bed at home and people would come to visit you. Then I had lots of pretty lacy nighties and little bed jackets which were lovely. Even the babies had frilly little nightdresses as they lay in their cots, which also had frills around them and which my mother had bought from Harrods. For each baby it was differently trimmed, blue for a boy and pink for a girl. The nursery maid used to have to spend hours washing and ironing the children's nightclothes and 'goffering' them which was crimping the collars to make frills. Of course it's all changed now, no one has the time to dress babies like that, and they are all put in very sensible little babygros.

Upgrade

These days if you want to be upgraded on a flight you probably need to be a social media influencer and you could just be wearing a fashionable pair of jeans, but back when my friend Margaret and I were flying to India we perfected the art of being upgraded. We realised you just needed to look and act the part. We were particularly successful on Canadian airlines, I don't know why but they seemed to like posh-looking people. We always wore a hat and gloves as someone once told me that you had to look as if you belonged in first class so that when you got there the other paying passengers didn't notice you. They wanted to feel as if everyone had paid for the seats like them. Canadian Airlines often seemed to overbook economy and we'd be there standing in the queue looking terribly smart and respectable, and we were often picked out to be bumped up – it was marvellous.

Vera Lynn

I knew Vera Lynn quite well as I was asked to be president of a disability charity she had founded in 1953. She'd asked lots of her celebrity friends to raise money to help children with cerebral palsy; it was a clever idea and a wonderful charity. I organised fundraising events for it with various famous people like Bob Hope and Sir John Mills. Vera had been such an icon during the war and had done so much to lift the spirits of servicemen, she was universally adored. But she was also pretty demanding, and at board meetings she attended, one had to watch one's P's and Q's. I remember being ticked off by her once or twice and found her slightly intimidating. She came back to haunt me recently when I was being interviewed by the etiquette expert William Hanson at Cheltenham Literary Festival about my book *Picnic Papers*. I first published the book in 1983 and it was very difficult trying to get hold of an original copy, but William had found one online from a second-hand bookseller and when he opened it, he discovered it was signed by me to Vera Lynn. I don't think I gave away many copies but I had clearly given one to her. It was as though she was still there watching over me, waiting to see if the new edition of *Picnic Papers* was up to scratch!

Visitors

There are all types of visitors, some you wish would stay longer and some you can't wait to be rid of. I think there are various rules to being a good guest or visitor. Firstly, think of an appropriate present to take for your host. If you don't know them very well then something like a nice tin of biscuits will do but if you know they like gardening perhaps find them an interesting or rare plant they might enjoy. When you arrive I think it's a good idea to ask to see where you are sleeping as it's quite nice to know where the bedroom is and how to get to it, and perhaps unpack a little to have a sense of settling in. And then the key to being a good guest is just to go along with whatever is planned; yes, you'd be thrilled to go to an old people's home to visit Great Aunt Gwen or be delighted to sit next to the chief of police at dinner. I've had my fair share of tricky visitors and it's a joy when you have someone who will fit in and be positive about what you have in store. I also love walking, so when I'm staying somewhere I'll often suggest going for a walk, perhaps taking the host's dog if that's helpful. In that way the host gets a bit of a breather, and everyone can relax for a couple of hours. When you return, hopefully there's a drink on offer and a whole new spate of conversation ensues. Being appreciative and undemanding is key.

I am not always a fan of the unexpected visitor. Sometimes quite out of the blue, I have people knocking on my door at home who might have a copy of my book to sign. Obviously, it's wonderful to have sold a book but quite often I might not be looking my best, and I won't have had my hair done. I have a quick look out of a window and grab one of my many hats lying nearby to jam onto my head before coming to the door. I do generally like to have some notice of visitors, but sometimes the unexpected is extremely welcome. The other day Christabel and Jools Holland called me as they were on their way to stay with the King but were early so they very kindly asked if they could take me out for lunch. We went to the Victoria pub at Holkham and had a delightful time.

Vodka

I've never drunk a tremendous amount, I like a glass or two at parties, but vodka is my favourite tipple. I think I like it because it goes with everything, although my staple mixer is tonic. It's also got less calories and sugar in it than other drinks. When the doctor asked me if I drank, I said, 'Yes, well up to a point!' I never drink in the evenings, but I do enjoy a vodka tonic at lunchtime. If the weather is nice I will repair to my hut in the garden, with a bowl of nuts or some popcorn, and sit there for half an hour or so with my vodka and nibbles and have a moment of real pleasure.

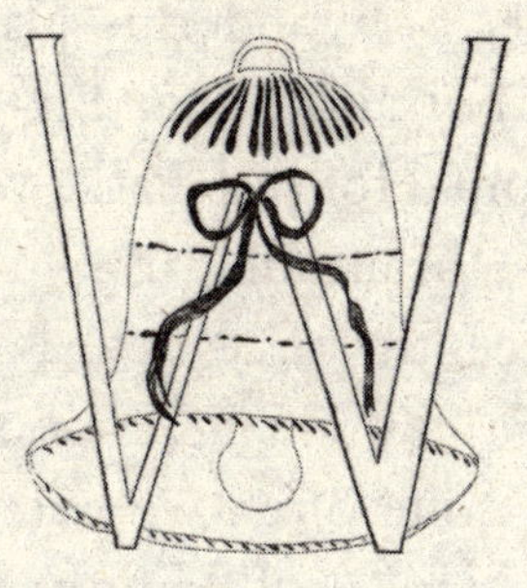

Walking

I think my love of walking came from my nanny Billy Williams. When we were in Scotland my sister and cousin, who were two years younger, were considered too young to walk long distances. I was only seven, but Billy used to take me on wonderful long walks by myself. She knew a great deal about plants and birds, and we'd take a notebook to write down what we had seen. They were happy times, and it was such beautiful countryside to enjoy. It gave me a love of walking, and I've walked every day since. I think it's so important to have a daily walk. Obviously as you get older you can't walk as far but I always at least try to do little rounds of the village.

There are lots of wonderful places to walk in North Norfolk but also when I'm in London I'm two minutes from Holland Park, which I think is one of the most beautiful parks in the city. When you are in the centre of it, it feels quite wild, and you can't believe you are in London. I'm a patron of the park and quite often we will raise money for a new tree or a statue, so I'll pop in and have a look at whatever is the latest acquisition. Especially in nice weather it's heartening to see so many people enjoying it, having picnics or playing games; it's very important to have these green spaces in London.

I've never been a doggy person, but I do think it would have been nice to have had a dog to take for walks. I did have a dog briefly once, years ago, a pug called Daphne, but she had terrible trouble breathing and it used to distress me, so I ended up giving her to Billy Williams who adored her. I'm always ready to take other people's dogs for walks, however, and my daughter and son-in-law have two dogs who I sometimes take out. Quite often I think it's them taking me for a walk as I'm dragged round on the end of the lead!

Waving

It's a slightly niche category this one, but having been lady-in-waiting, I did always notice the different ways in which members of the Royal Family waved. The Queen Mother did a stirring the pudding sort of wave, very graciously and very slowly. Princess Margaret had a rather more showy wave where she slowly waved her hand side on, and the Queen's wave was rather brisk, showing more of the front of her hand.

I found myself in something of a conundrum when I was on my way to the Coronation. I was in a car on my own as my mother had left earlier to have breakfast with the Queen at Buckingham Palace, before joining the procession in a coach. As I was driven to Westminster Abbey, all the people who had been camping in the rain all night were cheering at everything that went past, even the cleaners who arrived to clean the streets. Although they had no idea who I was they could see I was part of the Coronation as I was wearing my headdress, and I thought, *Should I wave or not?* I had no idea whether it was proper or whether I'd be reported by some furious man in the Queen's household for inappropriate waving. In the end I couldn't resist and did a tiny little wave, barely above the level of the car window.

I knew better than to wave when standing on the balcony at Buckingham Palace with the Queen later, no one made that faux pas. But it was incredibly difficult because when you see this huge crowd of people waving and cheering it's hard to resist. I had to make fists of my hands holding them down to remind myself not to do it.

On the windowsill in my kitchen at home I've got a tiny little statue of the Queen. She's holding a bag containing a solar panel which powers her to wave. Every time I make a cup of coffee, there she is sitting on the windowsill waving at me and it brings back all those lovely memories.

Weddings

Weddings these days are exhausting, sometimes they can go on for days, and often people seem to be having them abroad so that the guests are expected to pay for flights and somewhere to stay. I think it's all a bit much and can be very expensive both as a guest and to host. My daughter May was very kindly given permission to be married at Holkham, which was lovely, but even then I had to sell a piece of jewellery to pay for the whole thing. When I got married, my father organised a train to bring people up to Holkham from London, there was the church service, then a tea and then everyone went home. Colin and I left that night too. Quite often these days there's a dinner the night before, a long wedding involving lunch or dinner and then dancing, and often a lunch the following day.

My grandson Cody, who is the current Lord Glenconner, had a lovely wedding at Glen. The wedding service was in church in the morning, followed by a lunch and then, because I was staying in the house, I was able to nip up to my bedroom for a quick snooze before the evening. They had a ceilidh with a wonderful band and supper. It was great fun doing all the simple reels again, I had a lovely time and it was absolutely the right length.

Writing

Suddenly finding I had a career as a writer at the age of eighty-seven has been completely wonderful, but when it was first suggested I write a memoir I had to work out how to do it. I'm too old to write or type it myself but was told it was about capturing my voice, so I started with all my photograph albums, which prompted lots of memories, and I realised I had very good recall of events. Then I had to structure the book, working out what was going into each chapter. I would spend each morning talking into a digital tape recorder which then a writer called Hannah Bourne-Taylor would write up in the afternoon. In the evening we would go over what had been written and make any corrections that were necessary

What I hadn't expected was the flood of letters I received from all over the world. I've had people write to me from Russia, Australia, Ukraine and New Zealand, among others. I had a little card printed with my photograph on it and reply to every letter. Mostly I keep it quite brief, but I started receiving extremely heartrending letters, especially from people who were experiencing domestic abuse, and in those cases I write a proper letter back. At one point I was spending about an hour a day replying to fans' letters. Many of them were sent to Holkham and others just to Lady Glenconner, Norfolk or Norfolk Farmhouse, but the post office have been fantastic at getting them to me.

A paper recently asked me to write an agony aunt column but I'm far too old to take that sort of thing on and ill-equipped to deal with many of the awful things which people are coping with today. However, it is quite humbling to think that my experiences might have helped some people. The other day I had a letter from a woman who had lost her daughter who wrote that she keeps my book by her bedside. She said that she often wakes up sobbing in the middle of the night and then reads my chapter on grief and it helps her. It's very moving to think that the rather terrible things that have happened in my life I've been able to share in a way that is comforting to others in a similar situation.

X-rays

The most earth-shattering X-ray I had was when I was heavily pregnant with what I thought was my fourth child. The doctor was a bit worried because the baby's head hadn't engaged and I was thirty-eight, which in those days meant I was considered to be an old mother. It seems extraordinary now to think of doing an X-ray on a pregnant woman, but they didn't have all the amazing ultrasound technology that's available now. I had the X-ray and then went back to sit with the doctor when the nurse came running in waving the printout saying, 'Oh, Lady Anne, you are having twins!' I just burst into tears, it was utterly overwhelming, and I was so exhausted. The two babies were in the same sac but when I gave birth to them, one came out about three to four minutes before the second one and I remember the doctor saying, 'There you are, you have one little girl… and now another one.' I was completely thrilled.

Xenial

This is a word I've learnt recently that means, the hospitality shown towards guests, particularly those from another place, and it reminded me of the time I had Princess Elizabeth of Toro to stay. She was the incredibly elegant daughter of King George Rukidi III of Toro, a kingdom of Uganda. I first met her at the Coronation of the Kabaka of Buganda who had been a friend of Colin's at Oxford. I said to her that she should call me if she came to England. She was a very accomplished person, who had been only the third African woman admitted to Girton College Cambridge and then the first woman from East Africa to be admitted to the Bar. For a short time she was a foreign envoy and then Foreign Minister for Idi Amin following the overthrow of Milton Obote's government in 1971. But she fell out of favour with Amin and ended up in exile in the UK. She was very beautiful and clever and had a career as a model and an actress starring in the film of Chinua Achebe's *Things Fall Apart*. She came to stay with me in Norfolk when she was on her way to Cambridge.

It was lovely to see her, and we reminisced about the time Colin and I went to Uganda to visit her father in the late 1960s. We had gone at his invitation to visit the Pygmy tribe but her father, King George III had, unfortunately, always been drunk by about ten o'clock in the morning, so we never made the trip. I think she was rather exasperated by him.

Colin of course loved meeting people and inviting them to come and stay. My heart would slightly sink when he'd phone up and say, 'Oh, Anne, I'm bringing up so and so who've I've just met to come and stay.' Having heard she was a movie star, he'd introduced himself to Brooke Shields on a flight over from America and invited her up to Glen. She was very young and I was amazed that she would trust this man whom she had just met, but she came up with him straight off the plane. She phoned her mother from Glen, who I think gave her a bit of a rocket, but I overheard her saying what an amazing house it was, which I think helped at that point. She was lovely and the children thought she was great fun.

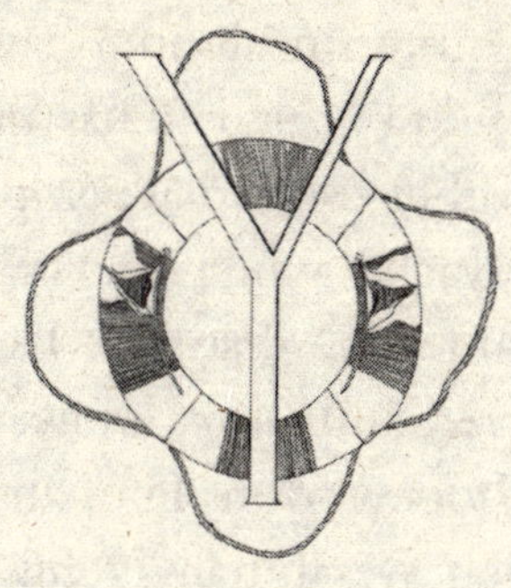

Yachting

There is a marvellous photograph taken of me on a yachting holiday where I am swimming in the sea but attached with a long lead to a member of staff on the boat, who is simultaneously walking a small dog on a lead around the deck. It was a wonderfully inventive solution to the dread I have about being swept out to sea on a strong tide, or some other disaster happening when I swim off the yacht belonging to a friend.

The only night I spent on the Royal Yacht *Britannia* was when I accompanied Princess Margaret to that reception for European Union Leaders in 1992, when it was docked in Edinburgh. It's still moored in Edinburgh and you can go on board and look round.

It was done up quite simply in a naval style, I think by the Duke of Edinburgh, and has a lovely, comfortable feel. My mother used to accompany the Queen, who loved the yacht, when she sailed in it round the Scottish islands. The first time I saw it was when Princess Margaret and Tony arrived in Mustique while on their honeymoon. They invited us onto it for dinner, which we initially refused on the basis that we hadn't had a bath in weeks and stank, but when they offered us a cabin on board with a bath, I think it was just about the best bath I'd ever had!

Zoom

I loathe Zoom. I sometimes have to use it, with my daughter-in-law's help, for interviews, but I always look absolutely hideous, no matter where I put the lights. And you have to pay attention to what is in the background, which suddenly seems so much more important than if you were sitting talking to someone in real life.

I recently did a speed awareness course on Zoom. I'm afraid I've had to do four speed awareness courses; it's the result of the impatience creeping in that I mentioned earlier. I've done two in person locally, which were an absolute nightmare, so boring, and took all day. I think we had to take along a packed lunch and they made us watch endless videos. The

Zoom course was rather better, despite my loathing of Zoom in general, as I could do it from home. I think there were around twenty of us online. We all looked like little postage stamps on the screen and a couple of people fell asleep almost immediately. I was asked when I'd passed my driving test and think they were a little taken aback when I said 1949. I was a real goody two shoes and absolutely thrilled to answer all the questions. It was one of the few Zoom sessions I'd quite enjoyed, plus it meant I didn't get points on my licence, so that was great. In fact, I have no points now which is good, and as I mainly just drive short distances these days, I'm hopeful it will stay that way.

Zest For Life

Now in my nineties, I think I'm having the most fun I've ever had in my life. There's so much to enjoy and look forward to. It's no longer the grand things that thrill me, it's the everyday pleasures: seeing the owls in flight that are nesting in my barn, having a drink outside with friends in my garden on a summer's day, browsing the fresh fruit and veg in my little greengrocer's, or spending time with my family. I've had a long and varied life, but I'm not finished yet. There are talks to give and book festivals to attend, and one of my friends has promised to take me for one last sail…

Acknowledgements

I would like to thank my daughter-in-law Johanna for all her invaluable help with this book, not just with recording my thoughts, but in helping with all the logistics involved with writing and promoting the book. Thanks also to my wonderful editor Sarah Harrison, we had such fun together and it's been a hugely enjoyable process. Thank you to the editorial team at Bedford Square Publishing, Jamie Hodder-Williams, Claudia Bullmore and Polly Halsey. And to Emma Draude and Katie Cregg at EDPR agency. I would also like to thank my agent Gordon Wise at Curtis Brown, and Philippa Gist for the wonderful illustrations.

About the Author

Lady Glenconner was born Lady Anne Coke in 1932, the eldest daughter of the 5th Earl of Leicester, and grew up in their ancestral estate at Holkham Hall in Norfolk. A Maid of Honour at the Queen's Coronation, she married Lord Glenconner in 1956. They had 5 children together of whom 3 survive. In 1958 she and her husband began to transform the island of Mustique into a paradise for the rich and famous. They granted a plot of land to Princess Margaret who built her favourite home there. She was appointed Lady-in-Waiting to Princess Margaret in 1971 and kept this role – accompanying her on many state occasions and foreign tours – until her death in 2002. Lord Glenconner died in 2010, leaving everything in his will to his former employee. Her bestselling memoir *Lady in Waiting* was published in 2019, and she has written bestselling fiction. She now lives in a farmhouse near Kings Lynn in Norfolk.

Picture Acknowledgements

Photographs Produced courtesy of:
Pg 1 Alban Donohoe
Pg 5 Bianca and Mick Jagger – Patrick Lichfield (via
    Getty Images)
All other photographs from the author's private
    collection

Every reasonable effort has been made to trace copyright holders, but if there are any errors or omissions, Bedford Square Publishers will be pleased to insert the appropriate acknowledgements in any subsequent printings or editions.

Bedford Square Publishers is an independent publisher of fiction and non-fiction, founded in 2022 in the historic streets of Bedford Square London and the sea mist shrouded green of Bedford Square Brighton.

Our goal is to discover irresistible stories and voices that illuminate our world.

We are passionate about connecting our authors to readers across the globe and our independence allows us to do this in original and nimble ways.

The team at Bedford Square Publishers has years of experience and we aim to use that knowledge and creative insight, alongside evolving technology, to reach the right readers for our books. From the ones who read a lot, to the ones who don't consider themselves readers, we aim to find those who will love our books and talk about them as much as we do.

We are hunting for vital new voices from all backgrounds – with books that take the reader to new places and transform perceptions of the world we live in.

Follow us on social media for the latest Bedford Square Publishers news.

🐦 @bedsqpublishers
⬤ facebook.com/bedfordsq.publishers/
⬤ @bedfordsq.publishers

https://bedfordsquarepublishers.co.uk/